ROUTLEDGE LIBRARY EDITIONS:
MILITARY AND NAVAL HISTORY

Volume 7

A HISTORY OF FIREARMS

T0332279

A HISTORY OF FIREARMS
From Earliest Times to 1914

W. Y. CARMAN

Routledge
Taylor & Francis Group

LONDON AND NEW YORK

First published in 1955

This edition first published in 2016
by Routledge
2 Park Square, Milton Park, Abingdon, Oxon OX14 4RN

and by Routledge
711 Third Avenue, New York, NY 10017

Routledge is an imprint of the Taylor & Francis Group, an informa business

British Library Cataloguing in Publication Data
A catalogue record for this book is available from the British Library

ISBN: 978-1-138-90784-3 (Set)
ISBN: 978-1-315-67905-1 (Set) (ebk)
ISBN: 978-1-138-92337-9 (Volume 7) (hbk)
ISBN: 978-1-138-92339-3 (Volume 7) (pbk)
ISBN: 978-1-315-68510-6 (Volume 7) (ebk)

Publisher's Note
The publisher has gone to great lengths to ensure the quality of this reprint but
points out that some imperfections in the original copies may be apparent.

Disclaimer
The publisher has made every effort to trace copyright holders and would welcome
correspondence from those they have been unable to trace.

A HISTORY OF FIREARMS

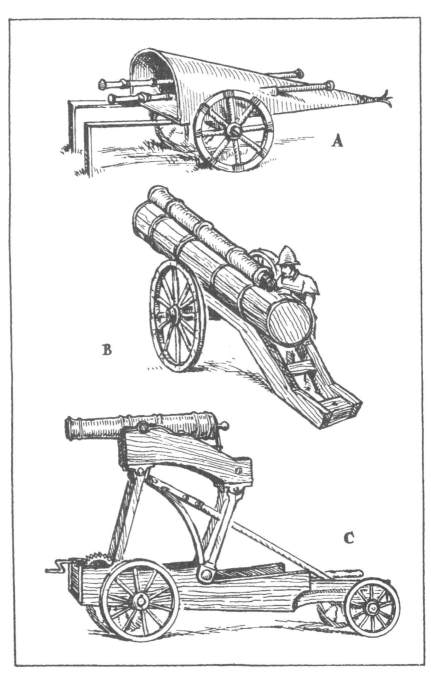

Frontispiece—A. Gun cart, 1544. B. 'The gun called Policy', 1544. C. Elevating carriage, eighteenth century.

A History of

FIREARMS

From Earliest Times

to 1914

by

W. Y. CARMAN,

F.S.A., F.R.Hist.S., F.S.A.(Scot.)

Keeper of Department of Exhibits Imperial War Museum

Routledge & Kegan Paul Ltd

LONDON

First published in 1955
by Routledge & Kegan Paul Limited
Broadway House, 68–74 Carter Lane,
London E.C.4

Second impression 1956
Third impression 1963
Fourth impression 1970

Printed offset in Great Britain
by The Camelot Press Ltd.,
London and Southampton

SBN 7100 1161 X

Contents

Illustrations

ACKNOWLEDGEMENTS

The staff of the Tower Armouries, the War Office Library and the Royal United Services Institution have been most helpful during research and are thanked gratefully for their willing co-operation.

Glossary

ARTILLERY—engines to throw projectiles by explosive or other means.

BARREL—the hollow tube of a gun or cannon.

BLOCK TRAIL—a trail which is made in a solid block.

BOLT—a short heavy arrow.

BOMBARD—from the Latin meaning 'hum'. Not necessarily a type or size of cannon.

BOMBARDELLE—a small bombard.

BORE—the hollow space inside the barrel, also the diameter.

BRAZIER—an iron basketwork to hold fire to heat cannon shot.

BREECH—part of the barrel which is open to take the charge.

CANNON—from 'cane', a tube. From early time referred to the heavier firearms.

CARBINE—a hand arm mainly used by cavalrymen, shorter than a musket.

CARRIAGE—the framework used to support and to transport a gun.

CASCABEL—the small projection at the rear end of the gun barrel.

CHARGE—the powder or propellent necessary to throw a shot.

CHASE—the part of the gun enclosing the bore.

COCK—apparatus for holding igniter, as in matchlock or flintlock.

COIGN—a wedge used for elevating or depressing a gun barrel.

DART—a heavy projectile shaped like an arrow.

DOG—another name for cock.

DOLPHIN—lifting handles so called because they were made as dolphins.

FELLOES—the piece of wood making the outer ring of a wheel.

FLAMMENWERFER—German flame thrower.

FLINTLOCK—a lock or apparatus to produce fire by means of flint.

FUZE—a device for igniting the charge in a shell, etc. The Oxford Dictionary gives 'Fusè' but 'Fuze' is the common 'Gunner' usage.

GIN—a wooden framework used for raising a gun barrel.

GUN—now taken to mean a weapon discharged by gunpowder but also said to have come from mangonel.

HOWITZER—a short gun firing shells at high angles.

IGNITERS—devices to ignite gunpowder or propellent.

LATON, LATONE, LATTEN—a yellow mixture like brass or bronze.

LIFTING HANDLES—attachments on metal gun barrel used to unship gun from carriage.

LIMBER—a two-wheeled contrivance to take the trail of gun carriage when on the move.

LOCK—a mechanism to hold means of ignition.

MAGAZINE—a storeplace of ammunition, a small compartment to hold ammunition.

MANGONEL—a type of wooden artillery.

MANTELET—a wooden shield to protect artillerymen during operations.

MATCH—length of cotton or other material impregnated to burn steadily.

MITRAILLEUSE—a generic name for French machine guns, from 'mitraille' small missiles.

MORTAR—a short wide-mouthed piece for throwing or lobbing projectiles.

MUZZLE—the front opening of a barrel or gun.

PAN—the hollowed portion of a lock used to hold the priming.

PRIMING—a small quantity of detonating compound necessary to set off the charge.

PROPELLENT—the means of propelling the projectile.

QUARREL—a short thick arrow often of metal, capable of being fired by gunpowder.

SPANNER—a lever or key used to wind up the spring in a wheel-lock.

STOCK—the wooden end or butt of a firearm.

TILLER—the wooden bed of a gun capable of being directed.

TOUCH HOLE—the hole through the barrel to the charge.

TRAIL—the long back portion of the carriage.

TRAIN—a group of artillery assembled for a specific purpose.

TRUNNION—projections on the side of a gun barrel to permit elevation.

WHEEL-LOCK—a lock worked by means of a spring, wheel and pyrites.

Introduction

The study of firearms can lead one through a vast range of inventions, and in trying to avoid going gradually away from the subject I have decided to limit my field to the strict definition as given by the *Oxford New English Dictionary* in which it is written that a firearm is 'a weapon from which missiles are propelled by the combustion of gunpowder or other explosive'.

So the narrow interpretation of firearms, as weapons to be carried in the hands or arms, is not accurate and the many varieties of heavy artillery should be included. Once again a definition is needed. Originally ancient artillery included such engines as giant slings, catapults, and espringals, but as the projectile was not shifted by means of an explosion, that branch of artillery is omitted from this work. Thus the major groups will include artillery of a heavy nature, mobile and immobile, lighter artillery including trench mortars; an even lighter group including machine guns which although portable by man are usually placed on the ground for firing; the slightly lighter group of those which are portable but need two hands as for the musket fired from the shoulder; and the last and lightest group, all those weapons carried in one hand such as the pistol and revolver.

If the subject is followed in decades and centuries, the slow development of heavy artillery at one period compared with the rapid changes in muskets seem to present an unbalanced picture; and a more or less continuous narrative dealing with one type of firearm at a time will probably give a smoother and more understandable story.

After grouping the normal firearms, there remain inventions which may begin in the limits of these definitions and then grow out of them. For example a rocket launcher might be considered as a firearm, but the rocket has developed into a self- or radio-controlled projectile not far removed from a re-mote-controlled aircraft, which can hardly be considered as a firearm. The many types of automatic pistols and carbines of the present era make for confusion. Thus it has been decided to limit this work to firearms in use up to the end of the First World War, and so avoid a short-sighted view from the present day; and this will allow the changing currents to be described without becoming involved in too many cross-references or too much confusing detail.

Closely allied with the weapon is the projectile and its propellent. These have a direct bearing on the development of firearms and we have therefore to study it carefully. So also, methods of igniting or detonating have an important part to play in the chain of events and these also are included.

The use of the word 'fire' in firearms has a literal interpretation as a noun rather than a verb. 'Explosive' arms might be a better term from some points of view but I would rather base this book on the usual word. So it will not be out of place to discuss the ancient use of fire because this led to the discovery of gunpowder, and later other propellents of better and stronger quality.

Torpedoes are omitted because the tube is the true weapon and as such it is uninteresting. Heavy bombs and block-busters are also the projectiles rather than the weapons, and therefore not included. Grenades and some types of bombs are included, for although they may be considered as projectiles they are at times fired from artillery and muskets. So much for the scope of the subject.

We cannot always tell who the earliest discoverers were. In some cases the development of a weapon or invention was so slow that several may have helped at important stages and yet not be individually of much interest. Dates are then more important, historically, than people.

The application of gunpowder to firearms took place at the end of a period known as the Dark Ages. The enlightened days of the Greeks and Romans had long since gone and most people were ignorant and superstitious. The learned class was the clergy, the monks who copied ancient manuscripts, who had the time to correspond with other learned men and to experiment in the intervals between religious practices, and who had the necessities of life supplied and did not have to strive constantly in the battle 'for existence. But even their search for knowledge was not without trouble. To possess knowledge of new processes and inventions in those days might bring the suspicion of being a magician or agent of the devil. Learned men were imprisoned for their possession of new learning—Friar Bacon was one, and even a Pope suffered this indignity. Thus it can be readily understood that many discoveries were not announced publicly for all to hear and know, but often hidden in enigmatic writings or not committed to paper at all. So the gradual release of the secret would come to mankind in a confused way with the record of the original author often lost. How different from our own times, when the inventor of a war engine is in the courts and newspapers for weeks while a government decides how much, and whether, he is to be paid. Rumour and legend gave names to inventors, often the wrong names.

But I have tried to trace the history of firearms and the pioneers who made that history, step by step from the first stages to the fringe of a complex modern science.

I

THE USE OF FIRE IN WAR

~~~~~~

I. EARLY EXPERIMENTS

THE modern use of the word 'firearm' brings to mind a weapon which expels a projectile by means of a sudden explosion; the 'fire' part of the word suggests the result of the exploded gunpowder. But long before gunpowder was invented fire and methods of using it had been employed in warfare.

It is true that the first application would be a direct method, such as when a raider applied a flaming torch to the wooden home of a helpless victim or to the inflammable portions of a fortress. The Assyrians and Ancient Greeks knew well how to use fire for both attack and defence, as may be learnt from bas-reliefs and the tales of Homer. The wielder of fire seeking per-sonal protection used various means of projecting the fire. Throwing a torch was elementary, but vessels or pots with inflammable mixtures, and a burning firehead to an arrow were soon developed. Even these had their defects. A Roman historian of the fourth century urges that such arrows must be shot gently, for a rapidly flying arrow would be extinguished by the displaced air.

It may be recollected that the Bible furnishes an early example of fire being conveyed by animals, on the occasion when Samson 'went and caught three hundred foxes and took firebrands and turned tail to tail, and put a firebrand in the midst between two tails. And when he had set the brands on fire, he let them go into the standing corn of the Philistines and burnt up the shocks, and also the standing corn, with the vineyards and olives.' In true Old Testament tradition, the Philistines retaliated also with fire and burnt the wife of Samson and his father-in-law.

An unusual means of producing fire was attributed to Archimedes—that at the siege of Syracuse, he successfully used large burning glasses to destroy the Roman ships. The Pharos at Alexandria, one of the Seven Wonders of the World, was also said to have had a large mirror at the top, which could be used to concentrate the rays of the sun and direct them to burn enemy rigging, even up to the distance of a hundred miles at sea, according to the exaggerated legends. In the Artillery Museum at Stockholm is an ancient burning mirror which may have been intended for something of the same ambitious purpose.

Experiments with such materials as oil, pitch, sulphur and other ingredients were all steps on the road to discover gunpowder, as will be seen later. Even the early crude mixtures added much to the terrors and difficulties of a besieged town. These wildfires were of a sticky nature which not only adhered to any object they hit, but spread and were difficult to put out, especially with water.

At the siege of Plataea in 429 B.C., the Plataeans were forced to put hides and skins over the woodwork of their fortifications to lessen the effect of the flaming missiles of the Peloponesian attackers. The Spartans on the same occasion used the combustible material in another way. They piled large bundles of wood against the city walls and after saturating them with a mixture of sulphur and pitch, set them on fire. This concoction could have hardly been the far-famed 'Greek fire', that could not be extinguished, for a sudden rainstorm put out the flames and saved the walls.

An invention for throwing liquid fire was used by the Boeotians at the siege of Delium in 424 B.C. Thucydides in his fourth book describes a hollowed tree trunk covered with iron. 'They sawed in two and scooped out a great beam from end to end and fitting it nicely together again like a pipe, hung by chains at one end, a cauldron. Now the beam was plated with iron and an iron tube joined it to the cauldron. This they brought up from a distance upon carts to the part of the wall principally composed of vines and timber and when it was near, inserted large bellows into the end of the beam and blew with them. The blast passing closely confined into the cauldron, which was filled with lighted coals, sulphur and pitch, made a great blaze and set fire to the wall. The defenders could not hold it and fled. In this way the fort was taken.' Fire from machines was also thrown at the siege of Syracuse 413 B.C. and at the siege of Rhodes 304 B.C.

New mixtures were being made to improve the qualities of the fire, and Æneas the tactician who lived about 350 B.C. has written down his recipe, where he tells us to 'take some pitch, sulphur, tow, manna, incense, and the parings of those gummy woods of which torches are made; set fire to the mixture and throw it against the object which you wish to reduce to ashes.' He also advocates egg-shaped containers which when lighted were to be thrown into enemy ships.

2. GREEK FIRE

Little advance seems to have been made in this field until the end of the seventh century A.D. Then appears the famous 'Greek fire', so long a terror to the enemies of the ancient Byzantine empire. So effective was it, that its composition became a state secret, with the direst penalties for whoever might reveal it. It is said that it was the invention of Kallenikos, an architect from Heliopolis or Baalbec in Syria. His semi-liquid mixture, known at the time as 'sea-fire' was exceedingly difficult to extinguish and water only served to make it more dangerous. This formula Kallenikos brought to the Emperor Constantine Pogonatus for him to use against the Arabs who at that time were besieging Constantinople, the chief city of Byzantium.

It was used with effect in the following year, A.D. 674 when the Saracenic fleet was destroyed by this new method. The Emperor had projecting tubes fitted to his fast sailing vessels and when the Greek fire was pumped through the tubes on to the woodwork of the enemy's shipping, it was most difficult to put out; vinegar, wine or sand were suggested as the only means.

3

Much effort was made to keep this invention a state secret, and it was not written down. The Emperor Constantine the Seventh, Porphyrogenitus, wrote to his son that he should 'above all things direct your care and attention to the liquid fire, which is thrown by means of a tube; and if the secret is dared to be asked of thee, as it has often been of me, thou must refuse and reject this prayer, stating that this fire had been shown and revealed by an angel to the great and holy Christian Emperor Constantine.' He made further dire threats to anyone who might reveal the secret to a foreign nation.

Further details of the methods of using this seafire in the late ninth century are given by Emperor Leo the Sixth, also called the Philosopher, who said that the artificial fire was to be discharged by means of siphons. The siphons were made of bronze and, placed in the prow of every war-vessel, were protected by wood. Leo the Sixth, in his *Tactics*, also tells his officers to use the small hand-tubes which had been lately invented, and when doing so to discharge them from behind iron shields.

It is a daughter of one of these Emperors, Princess Anna Commena who tells us much of these warlike inventions in her book on the life of her father, the Emperor Alexius the First, Commenus. In this work, the *Alexiad*, she stated that resinous gums from fir and other evergreen trees were to be powdered and mixed with sulphur. When the mixture was blown with powerful and steady breath through hollow canes or tubes and ignited at the tip of the tube, long jets of flame would sear the faces of the enemy like flashes of lightning. But the Princess leaves out important information, thus keeping in part the secret. Various learned men have guessed at the complete solution. Francis Grose in his *Military Antiquities* says the formula of her day was bitumen, sulphur and naphtha, but Colonel H. W. L. Hime in his *Origin of Gunpowder* suggests that the missing ingredient is quicklime. He points out that naphtha or anything in the petroleum class was not a normal product of Byzantium and had it been imported, especially from Arab or Saracen countries, its secret use would have soon been guessed. But quicklime could easily be produced in the building craft, without suspicion. And the effect of water upon it would only serve to raise the temperature.

A German writer in 1939, Albert Hausenstein, said that

successful modern experiments had been made with quicklime, sulphur and naphtha, but others in more recent times say that practical experience shows it *not* to work as the slaking of the quicklime would not be enough to vaporize and ignite the naphtha. The oil in the naphtha would envelope the quick-lime particles and prevent them from reacting with water. Direct ignition would, however, be effective. It seems that the secret may never be discovered, which is no great loss as the other developments of modern times leave in the category of playthings what was an epoch-shattering discovery, and pro-longed the life of the Byzantine empire for many extra years.

Anna Commena gives useful information about the tubes or siphons when she tells us that 'in the bow of each vessel the admiral put the heads of lions and other land animals, made of brass and iron, gilt, so as to be frightful to look at; and he arranged that from their mouths, which were open, should issue the fire to be delivered by the soldiers by means of the flexible apparatus.' The theory of siphons or pumps was well known in Greece and Rome where elementary fire-engines were employed against fires. The siphon on each ship was served by the two foremost rowers, one of whom was called the siphonator and his duty was to 'lay' the siphon. The weapon must have been on a swivel because in a sea-battle near the island of Rhodes in 1103, the Pisans were terrified by the apparatus which cast fire at them from all angles, even sideways and downwards. A report of the battle gives us full details. The first encounter of the Byzantine admiral was a fiasco, as he shot his fire too soon and missed the enemy vessel. The next in the fleet rammed a Pisan ship, fired at it and set it on fire. Then the successful attacker disengaged itself and caught three more of the enemy in the deadly blaze; after which the Pisan navy fled from the scene.

The small hand siphons may have been of two types. The first writer tells of a pellet which after being blown from a long hollow tube becomes ignited by a flame at the exit, while the other author describes the charge as projected by air. Bellows, blow-pipes or squirt would all seem to be possible methods of discharging the fire but it is difficult to decide which is meant, and the fanciful pictures of the period showing the fire-ships in action do not help to clarify this point. There is an illustration of a sea battle showing a ship with its blazing tube enveloping the enemy vessel in a mass of flames. This comes from a Greek manuscript of Skylitzes but very little can be learnt, for the fire-worker or siphonator leans in the bows with one hand on the tube, while his gaze is directed backwards.

1—Greek fire through syringe.

No other nation seems to have used the Byzantine secret fuel, and thus when the Crusades began in 1097 there were other imitations in the field, mainly based on the old mixture of sulphur, pitch or bitumen, and resin or other gummy substances, with the addition of naphtha or other ingredients. A metrical romance of Richard Cœur-de-Lion written in the reign of Edward the First, tells us that

> *King Richard oute of hys galye*
> *Caste wylde-fyr into the skye*
> *And fyr Gregeys into the see*
> *And al on fyr were the.*

Poetic licence seems to have given the King possession of the secret sea-fire but little evidence supports this.

Incidentally 'Greek fire' was not a term in use in either the Greek or Moslem languages and only dates from the time when the Christians came in contact with this liquid fire in the Crusades. No citizen of Byzantium would ever degrade himself or a compatriot by the name of Greek.

But Greek fire was dropping out of use and evidence of its presence after 1200 is lacking. The main reason for its disuse would appear to be that the Byzantines were no longer warlike and had become degenerate. In 1200, the commanding Admiral, Michael Struphnos sold the naval stores in Constantinople and 'turned into money not only the bolts and anchors of the ships but their sails and rigging and left the navy without a single large vessel.' The money he appropriated and the secret seems to have disappeared from this time. Four years later when members of the Fourth Crusade attacked their once-allied Christians in Constantinople, the sixteen war-ships had a poor variety of fire which the Venetians soon coped with.

The Saracens were not slow to use fire as a weapon against the Crusaders. At Acre, 1191, the Crusader siege towers were becoming too great a menace, so a Damascus metal worker produced a plan, which went as follows. 'First in order to deceive the Christians, he cast against one of the towers, pots with naphtha and other materials in an unkindled state, which had no effect whatever. Then the Christians took heart, climbed triumphantly to the highest story of the tower and assailed the faithful with mockeries. Meanwhile the man from Damascus waited until the stuff in the pots was well melted. When the moment had come, he slung anew a pot that was well alight. Straightway the fire laid hold on everything around, and the tower was destroyed. The conflagration was so violent that the infidels had not time to climb down. Men, weapons, everything was burnt up. Both the other towers were destroyed in a like manner.'

Even though this fire may not have been the genuine article as used by the Byzantines, it was sufficient to throw the Christians into great fear. Jean de Joinville, a later eye-witness of its effects, who wrote a *Histoire du Roy Saint Loys*, speaks of the terrors it effected among the commanders of St. Louis' army in 1249 at the siege of Darmetta. It was advised that as often as the fire was thrown, all should prostrate themselves on their elbows and knees and beseech the Lord to deliver them from that danger. But the results of this fire do not seem to have warranted this fear, because some of the attacking towers which had been set on fire were soon rescued from the flames. Joinville describes his experience in the following words. 'The Saracens brought an engine called a petrary and put Greek fire into the sling of the engine. The fashion of the Greek fire was such that it came front-wise as large as a barrel of verjuice

7

[a thirteenth-century flavouring sauce made from the juice of crab-apples] and the tail of fire that issued from it was as large as a large lance. The noise it made in coming was like Heaven's thunder. It had the seeming of a dragon flying through the air. It gave so great a light, because of the great poison of fire making the light, that one saw as clearly throughout the camp as if it had been day.' Mention of a large cross-bow being used four times to cast the fire shows that siphons or squirts were not in use, as they had been for the Byzantine fire. Geoffry de Vinesauf in his *Itinerari cum Regis Ricardi* (he accompanied King Richard I to the Crusades) says of the fire, the 'oleum incendiarium, quod vulgo Ignem Graecum nominant' that 'with a pernicious stench and livid flame, it consumes even flint and iron, nor could it be extinguished by water; but by sprinkling sand on it, the violence of it may be abated, and vinegar poured on it will put it out.'

The type of machine for throwing these barrels of fire could be of the principle of tension (large bows), torsion (twisted rope) or counterpoise (a weight at the end of a swivelled arm). Constant reference to the use of this artillery in European and Asiatic warfare, especially in the flowery language which spoke of thunder and lightning, may have led to the confusion in more modern writers' minds, that firearms and cannon were in use much earlier than was actually so.

A use of fire in Europe is recorded by Roger de Hoveden, who notes that it was used by Philip Augustus King of France to burn the English shipping in the harbour of Dieppe during a siege in 1193. This monarch had found a quantity of the inflammable material already prepared when he entered Acre and he did not hesitate to bring it to Europe to use against his fellow Christians. Even Edward the First ordered the employment of fire against the Scots at the siege of Stirling Castle in 1304. Fifteen years later a Flemish engineer, Crab, defended Berwick when besieged by Edward the Second, by means of a fiery mixture containing pitch, tar, fat, brimstone and the refuse of flax.

John Ardenne, a surgeon of the time of Edward the Third, proposed that apart from long-bows and cross-bows carrying an incendiary material, birds and animals could carry the fiery composition in iron or brass containers. A manuscript in the

Hauslaub Collection in Vienna illustrates a dog in a scaled coat with a spike and a flaming pot on his back pounding forwards to the enemy. A cat and a flying bird are also shown as pressed into this dangerous and uncomfortable service.

2—Fire carried by dog and bird, Middle Ages.

A French manuscript of the fourteenth century shows a large ballista slinging a barrel of flaming material at the enemy while another page of the same manuscript depicts a horseman in armour charging forward with a lance having a blazing head.

On the continent when the garrison of Ypres was besieged in 1383 by the Bishop of Norwich, the French successfully defended themselves by means of stones, arrows, lances, so-called Greek fire, and other missiles so that the English abandoned the siege leaving their cannon behind. The same English were soon after besieged in the town of Burburgh by the French who threw into it such quantities of fire composition, that they burnt one third of the town and forced the English to surrender.

At the siege of Damietta in 1249, Matthew Paris remarks that the fiery darts carried small containers filled with quicklime. English archers of the same period are said to have had the *spicula ignita*, or arrows tipped with wildfire. These were noted as part of the stores in Newhaven and Berwick in 1547. There were certain types of bows known as slur-bows which were ordered to be purchased in November 1588 and the projectiles to go with them were twenty dozen of firework arrows at five shillings per dozen. Sir John Hawkins advocates the use of fire-arrows in his book, the *Voyage into the South Sea*, 1593, and writes that 'to tease or spoyle the enemie's tackling and sails' arrows of fire were to be shot out of slur-bows. In a list of naval stores for 1599, long-bow arrows with fireworks were in store as well as slur-bow arrows with fireworks.

Even simple baked earthen jugs were made into offensive missiles, for a Frankfurt book of 1573 directs that they were to be filled with ashes and powdered quicklime. Then they were to be thrown against the enemy.

The Calendar of State Papers, Domestic Series, lists among the ammunition, supplied to the troops under Lord Lennox, who went to Scotland in 1545, the unusual item of 'xx tronckes charged with wild fyer'. An illustration of these 'tronckes' or 'trombes' is given in a book of 1560, P. Whitehorne's *Certain Waies for the ordering of Souldiers in Battelray*. They are shown as hollow wooden cylinders 'as bigge as a man's thigh and the length of an ell' and were filled with a mixture of sulphur, charcoal, pitch, turpentine, bay salt and saltpetre. It is this saltpetre that made a revolution in the many experiments of these early days, for it was its use in a purified form in the various fire-compounds that led to the discovery of gunpowder.

Fire-pikes were used in the English Civil War. Prince Rupert in his Journal records that when Bristol was being besieged by the Royalists in 1643, 'Lieutenant-Colonel Littleton (of Bowle's Regiment) riding along the inside of the line with a fire-pike, quite cleared the place of defenders; some of them crying out "wild-fire". Thus was the line cleared for a great way together.' Later when some musketeers failed to dislodge a defending party 'Captain Clerk, Ancient Hodgkinson and some others rushing upon them with fire-pikes, neither men nor horses were able to endure it. These fire-pikes did the feat.'

A French engineer, Gambert of Mante, boasted that he had rediscovered the secret of making Greek fire but Francis Grose, the antiquarian, says that luckily for mankind it has since been lost. Grose also speaks of chemists in Britain, France and Holland who had found a like secret, but the governments of those countries for humanitarian reasons suppressed the information. There was a Roman named Poli who in 1702 invented a 'perilous fire', the secret of which was bought by Louis the Fourteenth, for no other reason than to have it suppressed. In the same year the Prussian army had a Schlangen-Brand-spritze, a serpent fire-spray, which its inventor P. Lange said would throw a mass of flame and fire twelve feet wide and forty paces long. Two sprays were capable of defending a breach and the whole apparatus was so light that four men could carry it. It could also be used at sea to set enemy shipping on fire; or as an afterthought, it was suggested that it could be filled with water and used to put out a fire. But by 1704 the invention seems to have been abandoned, no doubt because it failed to reach its high expectations.

Another French engineer, Dupré, in 1753 was said to have invented an inflammable liquid on the lines of Greek fire. Three years later it was put to the test when it was sprayed from a pump on to a sloop in Le Havre harbour and set the ship on fire. It was suggested that the invention should be used against the English when they were bombarding Le Havre the next year but the Royal Authority for its use was not forthcoming.

Fire was used in warfare in the nineteenth century. The Red Indians in America had for some time used fire-arrows against the white settlers and this weapon was also employed by the Chinese as late as 1860 against the French. These simple methods were not sufficient for the Americans during their Civil War and they produced a type of 'Greek fire' which they used in tin tubes. The solid mixture contained phosphorus, sulphur and carbon. But a fiercer ingredient was coming into popular use.

3. PETROLEUM AND NAPHTHA

Petroleum was known in ancient times and its name shows its origin—oil from rock. Naphtha is another ancient term having reference to the earth origin of the oil This natural material came to the notice of the western world when Alexander the Great led the Greeks into Persia. The hero had little practical knowledge of its properties but Plutarch knew of its explosive nature and said that it was like bitumen and could be set on fire without being touched, by means of the rays sent forth from a fire burning the air which was between both. Naphtha and petroleum, extracted from the earth are both well known for their volatile properties.

Naphtha is an ingredient in a recipe of 'Greek fire' in A.D.

350, which included sulphur, bitumen, and resin and was de-scribed by Vegitius in his *De Re Militari*. Flaming naphtha was used extensively in Arab warfare. When the Ka'aba was burnt down during the siege of Mecca in 683 it was the Syrians who were said to have been responsible by using burning naphtha. When stones slung from ballistic machines failed to quell the defenders of Heraclea in 805, Sultan Harun ar Raschid ordered incendiary material to be used, which soon brought about the surrender of the terror-stricken garrison.

An extraordinary device, where both horse and rider were used as a weapon or vehicle of fire, was employed on an occa-sion against the Mongols in 1256 by the Egyptians. The de-scription is awe-inspiring even to the reader. 'Having throughly soaked his shirt, the rider puts on a doublet of felt treated with a protective mixture (vinegar, red clay, dissolved talc, fish glue and sanderac) also soaked. The horse is covered with a caparison of the same. To the doublet are attached bells, and little madfaa (powder boxes) with fuses attached. The rider wears a helmet covered with felt soaked in naphtha and wisps of tow dipped in naphtha are attached to the doublet. Having rubbed his hands in talc powder he goes into action, preferably by night, carrying a lance dipped in naphtha or some incendiary composition which he whirls around and around—and accom-panied by foot men who carry clubs for sprinkling naphtha.' As an afterthought it is said that 'the horse must be first con-siderably accustomed to the noise and the glare'. The amazing effect of the burning horse and man is said to have achieved its result and routed the Mongol cavalry, but on a later occasion the performance was a failure because the flames died down before the fiery rider reached his objective.

Caxton in his *Myrrour and Description of the Worlde*, 1480, writes of 'another fountayne there is towarde the Oryent where-of is made fyre grekysshe with outher myxtyons that is put thereto, the which fyre when it is taken and lyght is so hote that it cannot be quenched with water.' He stated that the Saracens sold 'this water dere, and derer than they do good wyne''. Balls of naphtha were used in India and thrown by means of catapults, and one account tells us that the howdah of a noble-man who was riding on an elephant became set alight.

The troops at the siege of Charleston in America in 1863

used coal naphtha in shells and also obtained striking results by pumping it through hoses. Monsieur Berthelot commented on the effect of fire thrown into Paris by German guns during the siege of 1870. He advocated the repulse of the enemy by means of pumps throwing jets of burning petrol. The idea was adopted and although an apparatus was completed by 1871 it was not used against the enemy. As the writer bitterly remarked, its only use was by the French Commune against its own nation for the purpose of destroying public buildings and and palaces.

The Germans had it in mind to use petrol for warfare and early in the twentieth century during manœuvres a German officer claimed to have repulsed an attack on his stronghold by means of pressing the fire brigade into action. When he was not taken seriously, he said that on the proper occasion he would have used petrol instead of water in the hoses. This may have encouraged the Germans to experiment secretly but it was the work of Leidlet, a Belgian, that led to the introduction of the *flammenwerfer*. There is a captured German document of 12th December 1915, which states that *flammenwerfer* were a new weapon to be used in trench warfare. The 3rd Guard Pioneer Battalion consisting of six companies had been equipped with this invention which was to be used in two forms. The larger version of which there were twenty to twenty-two per company, were to be built in bastions and other defended places and could throw a fiery jet 33 to 44 yards. Each company also had eighteen small portable projectors which were to be carried on one's back and could throw their flames 16 to 19 yards.

The first use of the *flammenwerfer* was in a dramatic surprise attack on the French at Melancourt, 26th February 1915. Their first employment against the British was in July of the same year on the Ypres salient near the village of Hooge. The attack was successful but a few days later a counter-attack saw the capture of two *flammenwerfer*. These had a cylinder about two feet high divided into an upper chamber with nitrogen under compression and an oil reservoir. The oil coming up under pressure was ignited by a friction lighter in the nozzle of the short hose.

In June of the following year, 'Z' company of the Special Brigade went to France with flame-throwers, sixteen of which were portable and four of a larger type. Two of the large type were used successfully against the Germans in an attack on the Somme on 1st July. Underground galleries had been dug in the direction of the German trenches, and at the moment for the attack the nozzles were thrust about a yard into the air and threw flames about 900 yards, soon clearing the enemy trench. It took a ton of oil for each 'shot' and the cumbersomeness of the weapons prevented frequent use. Smaller types were occasionally used but the danger to the carrier, who had to be within twenty yards of his objective, brought the story that in the German Army operators were found by means of punishment.

During the First World War, it was intended to use flame-throwers in the Navy, and H.M.S. *Vindictive*, one of the storm ships for the attack on Zeebrugge Mole in April 1918, had two large machines built on the port side of the ship. The apparatus was very cumbersome, as may be seen from one of the remaining projectors still preserved in the Imperial War Museum. Unfortunately enemy shellfire damaged the projectors before they could get into action. One operator, not knowing that his igniting section had been shot away, carried on the action but instead of fire just pumped oil at the Mole.

The use of flame did not die out after that war, for the Italians found it of value to use against the Abyssinians. The Spanish Civil War proved its use even on tanks where flakes flew off inside the armoured vehicle to the detriment of the crew. 'Molotov' cocktails were an extempore use of petrol, very reminiscent of the early fire pots. But the modern development of petrol warfare including the man-carried 'Lifebuoy', the 'Wasp' and 'Crocodile' are all outside the sphere of the present work and must be studied elsewhere.

II

THE DEVELOPMENT OF CANNON

~~~~~~

I. EARLY EXPERIMENTS

To find the inventor of the first cannon is an impossible task, but most authorities agree that it is not Father Schwartz despite the fact that he is commemorated as such in stained glass. The date of his discovery has sometimes been given as 1354. But evidence exists for weapons fired by gunpowder as early as 1324 and they may well have been in use earlier.

There is an unsubstantiated claim that guns were made in Germany in the year 1313 and this must be examined to determine its value, if any. The statement first appears in the Memorial Books of the Town of Ghent and reads 'Item, in dit jaer was aldereerst ghevonden im Deutschland het ghebruk der bussen van einem mueniuck.' (In this year were guns designed by a monk in Germany.) Sir Charles Oman examined this subject in a most critical manner and when he was in Ghent in 1923 he had the active assistance of Dr. Bergmann, the Librarian of the University Library, to look into this point. The particular entry occurs only in the body of the later editions of the book. In the earlier ones it is inserted in the margin and in the handwriting of the early sixteenth century or even later. Thus this is not contemporary evidence and the most important point is that the earliest copy to have the note has the date of the year not 1313 but 1393! Perhaps some copyist transcribed MCCCXCIII as MCCCXIII but in any case the evidence is valueless.

Sir Charles Oman in his *Art of War in the Middle Ages* writes of an anonymous Arabic manuscript also on the art of war, which in pre-Bolshevik days was in the Asiatic Museum at St. Petersburg. In this, artillery which used gunpowder is described, and the methods used were so crude that Sir Charles was inclined to place this document at the beginning of the fourteenth century, especially as the last historical date in the manuscript was that of a battle in 1304. The early firearm is described as a *madfaa*, a term still in use for a cannon in eastern countries. It was in the shape of a hollow cylindrical log of wood, short like a mortar and wider at the top than the bottom. Its bore was to be filled half-way up with primitive gunpowder of the proportions, three of sulphur, four of charcoal and twenty of saltpetre. It was to be tamped down with a wad. If more than half filled with powder, it was suggested that it would burst. One has doubts in any case. The cannon ball was to be larger than the muzzle, placed on top, as Sir Charles says, like an egg on an egg-cup. The powder was to be ignited at a touch-hole. These are such extraordinary ideas that one wonders if the writing is not by an ignorant Arab after having a hearsay account brought to him.

The same writer describes another invention for shooting with either bolts or very small balls. This was a tube, some five inches broad, in which was placed an iron case (also called a *madfaa*). A quantity of gunpowder was placed below the iron case at the bottom of the tube and the ball or bolt was placed in the iron case. When the charge exploded the case carried the projectile forward, but to prevent the case being lost, one was instructed to tie the case to the tube by means of a strong silk cord. A cord that stood up to such explosions must have been very strong or the charge very weak—in which case the projectile would have gone nowhere. With correction these accounts could apply to mortars and chambered cannon but the point is that the Arab writer did not understand the art of gunnery and makes us doubt the ancient knowledge of gunpowder in the east.

Practical evidence of the use of cannon constantly comes back to Europe. On the continent the tradition is strong that a German monk was the father of artillery. Because he was referred to as *niger Bertholdus* or *der schwarze Berthold* some have referred to him as a black man, in keeping with the tradition that the invention came from outside Europe, but the black refers to his monkish dress, possibly that of a Franciscan. Roger Bacon who wrote so much openly and secretly on the subject of gunpowder before it was generally used, was a Franciscan. Thus there would be an early opportunity for the brothers of a fraternity, even over long distances, to exchange information on such an unusual subject. It is true that the most substantial evidence of Father Schwartz does not appear to date before 1400 but at that time a German manuscript tells of 'an maister der heiss niger Perchtoldus und ist gewesen ein nygramantikus'.

Details of his life grow with the passing of centuries and as fresh writers take up the tale. The popular story of his discovery according to an eighteenth-century book says that Bartold Schwartz (now using the 'black' of his robe as a surname) a monk of Mentz (others give Friburg) in 1320 discovered by accident the use of gunpowder. He happened to mix some saltpetre with sulphur in a mortar and covered it with a stone. The composition took fire—how is not explained—and the explosion blew the stone a considerable distance. This suggested 'the notion, that if this composition was properly confined, it might be useful in the attack and defence of places'. Another version says that while Schwartz was pounding the ingredients a spark from the laboratory fire set off the mixture. The resultant explosion shattered the mortar and threw the pieces at a distance. Some accounts give 1313 as the date of discovery but the Ghent accounts seem to shake this 'evidence' and most of the details of Father Schwartz seem to have been compiled centuries after his supposed life. While we have contemporary evidence of monkish knowledge of gunpowder, the truth of its application to firearms is not so clear.

It is interesting to note that the earliest illustration of a gun, that can be authenticated, is in an English manuscript. In the library of Christ Church, Oxford, is an illuminated Latin manuscript called 'De Officiis Regum'—on the Duties of Kings —which was dedicated by Walter de Millemete to Edward III. The writer had been tutor to Edward and the book is dated 1326 (1327 according to our present reckoning) the year of Edward the Second's murder. Unfortunately the text makes no reference to the illustrations and one must take the picture for what it is. The firearm is shown as a large vase or pot lying on its side. A short and heavy arrow is leaving the aperture and the knight has just ignited the gunpowder by means of a red-hot piece of metal applied to a hole in the side of the weapon. The missile, possibly an all-metal bolt, is directed against a castle doorway.

The shape of the firearm may be thought extraordinary but the term *vasii* was used extensively in the early days by the Italians as was the term *pot-de-fer* by the French. The pot in the illustration has a long narrow neck and is depicted resting on a platform without any device to counteract the recoil. The dart might be of iron with imitation feathers and it is difficult to see how the explosion could drive it out without a wad, but the artist may not have thought it necessary to show this. We are also faced with the possibility that the artist may have reconstructed the weapon from written or other description and was hazy on practical details.

Modern writers have 'seen' the mention of gunpowder in many of the old documents, especially the Oriental writings. A United States Government book as recent as 1949-put the invention of gunpowder as early as the ninth century and fire-arms at 1118, but needless to say without supporting evidence and no mention of that important ingredient, saltpetre.

The difficulty is to decide when cannons were first used. Absolutely contemporary evidence is scrappy and accounts slightly later are quite generous in giving cannon to their an-cestors. A later statement is not necessarily evidence but it is generally accepted that guns were used at a siege of Metz in 1324, although it is a later account which says that *serpentine et canons* were the weapons. An account of the Arabs at the siege of Bassetta in 1325 where they used machines casting forth globes of fire with the sound of thunder need not refer to cannon and gunpowder but rather to slings and naphtha balls, if one takes into account the exaggerated and poetic nature of Oriental descriptions.

A Florentine manuscript of 1326—the Rinformazione di Firenze—would appear to be correct with its details of metal cannon and iron darts and balls. The mention of the word cannon is a very early one and shows the antiquity of this type of firearm but before we go on to discuss the cannon in detail, there are other references to be mentioned.

Many writers assume that the first use of cannons was by the English in 1327 and quote *The Brus* as evidence. This poetical work was produced by Archdeacon Barbour of Aberdeen who lived from *c.* 1316 to 1395 and his writing has all the ring of truth. The engagement of the Scots under Douglas with the English took place at Weardale in August 1327 and the poet-clergyman wrote of the occasion:

> *Twa noveltys that dai thai saw*
> *That forourth in Scotland had been nane*
> *Tymbris for helmys war the tane—*
> *The tathyr crakys war of wer*
> *that thai before herd never er.*

Edward the Third was accompanied on the campaign by John of Hainault and Flemish troops who could have brought something new from the continent. The first novelty that the Scots had not seen was 'tymbris' or crests for helmets. The second was 'crakys of wer' and what these were must be determined. Barbour was careful to point out that at an earlier battle, Berwick 1319, Crab the engineer 'gynis for crakys had he nane'. 'Crakys' were of no use without 'gynis' and thus crakys were not guns but part of something. The old 'fire-books' written before gunpowder came in use had recipes for rockets, Greek fire and crackers. These crackers would appear to be the answer and they were not propelled by explosives but thrown by gins, gyns or guns, and produced a terror-making effect. The term gun is said to have been derived from gonne, gynnis, or mangonel, an engine in use previously. Examples of old names used for new inventions are common, and the ribaudequin was originally a spear-carrying cart but later a firearm. This makes for interest but also for difficulty in determining where the change of application takes place.

In 1331 the Italians, in Cividale in Friuti, were besieged by German troops who used *vasa e scioppi*. The possibility of the vases being incendiary ones is rendered remote by the employment of the *scioppi* which are definitely firearms.

A document of 11th July 1338 in the Bibliothèque Nationale Paris shows that the French Arsenal at Rouen issued for use against the English an iron pot to fire quarrels. Issued at the same time were forty-eight of these arrows which were iron and 'feathered'. One theorist has calculated that each iron arrow or quarrel would weigh a quarter of a kilogramme or about seven ounces. These pots and vases were passing out of fashion and it may be that they evolved into something in the way of mortars.

To return to the cannon, which is the main line of larger firearms. The word 'cannon' is said to come from *canna*, 'cane', a reed, although Demmin states the derivation is *kanne*, German for a drinking vessel. The canna or reed had been in use previously for the discharge of Greek fire and seems more probable than a drinking can. The making of a cannon was not a simple proposition. To achieve the shape a wooden core or mandrel was necessary. On this long bars of iron were temporarily fixed. Then over these at intervals iron rings were shrunk on. From this method of construction, it can easily be seen why the result was and is referred to as a barrel, for the same method of rings or hoops placed over bars of staves was used. White heat was necessary to weld the segments into a solid mass after which the wood was extracted or burnt. It can be seen that weaknesses were bound to occur in this method of manufacture. At a later date, cannon were cast solid and the centre had to be 'bored' out. But the barrel method of construction made a tube open at both ends. Thus more or less by accident, the first cannon was a breech-loader, as opposed to the mortar which usually was a muzzle-loader.

The large barrel of the cannon was lashed or chained to a firm wooden bed. The wood was usually carried separately and built into the ground at the appropriate place near the fixed target. The right angle of sighting also had to be built before the metal cannon was slung into position. At the rear end further upright blocks of wood were driven into the ground or firmly attached to the bed. In the small remaining space between the end of the gun and the upright blocks was placed the chamber or breech. This chamber was the receptacle to hold the powder and shot made ready for firing. The chamber was then placed with the open end continuing the bore of the barrel and further wooden wedges were driven in to keep it firmly to a close fit. The chamber or breech-piece was usually

3—Breech-loading cannon, 1417.

forged out of a single ingot and quite strong. The barrel acted as a guide for the shot to go on its allotted task. Several breech-pieces could be used and the shot made ready in advance. The principle had much in its favour. The weakness was the join between the chamber and the piece. It is curious to note that long after this type of ordnance disappeared, the chambers continued in use. As late as the nineteenth century, at the Tower of London, twenty chambers were loaded and fired when the necessity arose for a forty-one gun salute as on Royal occasions.

The method of forging cannon led to large cannon being made and these were, of course, cumbersome. The brass and other founders sought their own solution. We know that small firearms were cast, but the necessity for larger items made the craftsman improve his work and cast cannon were not slow in appearing.

Whether the cannon paid for in 1338 French accounts by the War Treasurer, Barthelmy du Drach, was cast is not known; but further French accounts for Cambrai on 8th October 1339 for ten cannon, five of iron and five of metal for the defence of that city lead us to think that they were in production.

2. ENGLISH ARTILLERY ON THE CONTINENT

England soon acquired cast cannon and an inventory of warlike stores kept for the defence of the City of London in the reign of Edward the Third against an expected French invasion lists six instruments of latone called gonnes and five roleres to the same. There were also lead pellets in store for these guns. It is suggested that a Florentine business company had them brought to the City where they were stored in the Guildhall. According to a chronicle written at Sluys the English navy used guns for the first time at the Battle of Sluys in 1340 but little opportunity arose for any striking results. These cannon must have been cast, for the larger versions would not have fitted on the vessels in use at the time.

By now references to cannon were widespread. Froissart in reporting the attack on the town of Quesnoi by the French in 1340 makes his first reference to cannon. The defenders of the town fired cannons and bombards which threw large quarrels. An account of the same date, preserved in the Archives of the Town Hall of Lille, quoted payment to Jehan de Fur for 'IIII tuiau de tonnoire et pour cent garros—VI livres XVI sous'. The small cost, only a little dearer than those of Cambrai, of the four thundering pipes and the hundred quarrels seem to indicate weapons of small size. The Lille accounts for 1341 record another piece which is called a small 'bouche a feu' about a hundred pounds in weight.

In 1340 Froissart also stated that firearms were used effectively at the siege of Tournoi. As they were for defensive purposes they may have been something in the ribaudequin line, but the besiegers drew off because they feared harm to their horses—either a considerate thought or a good excuse. Brass or copper soon became a popular metal for artillery despite the fact that it was expensive by the prices of those days. William a brazier of Aldgate in 1353 cast four guns of copper for King Edward the Third. Their cost seems low at thirteen shillings and fourpence each, but another gun of latten (a brass mixture) was made by Peter the Joiner for one pound. Iron by reason of its cheapness became more and more popular but at the beginning was not easy to cast in such a large size. A little later they are found not only in the arsenals of the Tower of

London and Calais (then English) but at most castles of importance around the country. It was the improvement in the art of
casting guns which permitted stronger gunpowder to be used.
This risk could not have been taken in the old 'staved' type of
gun-barrel.

Before we go any farther there is one subject which has
raised great controversy, and may continue to do so. It is,
whether or no the English had guns at the battle of Crécy, 1346.
It is striking that for such a famous battle the information now
preserved permits so much doubt, and that the case for and
against should have debatable points. Taking the evidence of
the foremost contemporary chronicler, we find that Froissart
was only eight or nine years old at the time of the battle and
must have relied on the evidence of others given at a much
later date. Some versions of his chronicles do not mention
cannon for this occasion but an Amiens transcript of *c.* 1378
does, and so also a later Abrège by the same writer speaks of
the English 'loosing off two or three bombards'. Two contemporary Italian accounts mention the English guns. One of these,
by Villani who died in 1348, speaks of *pelloti* being cast by
means of fire and the other, the *Istorie Pistolesi*, tells of many
bombards. Discreditors say that Froissart added cannons much
later and that the Italians only produced the cannons to excuse
the defeated Genoese. Contemporary evidence, however, cannot be ignored.

Factual evidence from bills for payment etc., show that gunpowder was being made for King Edward the Third before the
battle and that he had at least twenty guns at the siege of Calais
which immediately followed the battle of Crécy. The invention
of cannon cannot be denied but the point of contention is that
cannon at that time were normally used for siege work because
they had to be built on their carriages *in situ* and were not
mobile on a battlefield. A fixed line of fire would be of no
value against a rapidly moving enemy but there were other
firearms apart from the large cannon. The smaller cast cannon
of brazen mixtures could have been available and the wheeled
ribaudequins were most probable. Each of these two-wheeled
carriages had a number of small tubes. If they had been used at
Crécy that would account for the apparent discrepancies—the
many bombards of the Italian version meaning many small

barrels, and the two or three guns of Froissart meaning separate carts. The *pelloti* or pellots quoted by Villani would be the right ammunition for ribaudequins and we know that Peter van Vullaere a *maitre des ribaudequins* at Bruges in 1339 took service with the English force. The *bombardeaux* or little bombards of ancient accounts could easily be his.

Another point arises from this—if Villani can be accepted for Crécy—he was a trustworthy banker—then his statement that Lord Derby used iron guns when besieging Monsegur for fifteen days in 1345 will put the English claim for artillery back to an earlier date. Of course in this case it is siege rather than field artillery which is intended.

From the Pipe Rolls of the Exchequer 1344 to 1351 come details of stores for the King's war with France. One order of 1st February, 1345 was for 'gunnis cum sagittis et pellotis', (guns with arrows and pellots). Another on the 4th March 1346 was for 'gunnis cum pelotes et pulvere pro eisden gunnis' (the powder with the guns mentioned on this occasion can only be gunpowder). Then on the 10th May 1346 were recorded ten guns on stocks or beds, six pieces of lead, five barrels of powder and one hundred large pellots. All these were to be shipped for the King's use. Actually Edward the Third landed at La Hoque 12th July 1346. The circumstantial evidence of artillery is available all around the controversial period. It is a pity that the statement of artillery at Crécy is not permitted to stand without challenge.

There is a manuscript by Wetewange in the Bodleian Library at Oxford which gives a list of the forces laying siege to Calais late in 1346. These include a group of 314 men who are described as 'cementarii, carpentarii, fabri, ingeniatores, armatores, gunnatores et Artile' who were paid at the rate of 12d., 10d., 6d. and 3d. per day which were not low rates of pay.

The accounts of Laon 1356 give note of an improvement. Among the many pieces of artillery which are listed is one called 'a large cannon with a tail'. It still fired quarrels with oaken staves and was small, by later standards. The same accounts also give mention of another idea; twenty-four cannons were to be placed on tripods. This type of carriage is a striking advance and it may be that the tail to the gun was used to depress it when placed on one of these tripods. Another innovation is a plate of metal to cover the touch-hole. For all these developments, these accounts include details of the old wooden artillery, espringals and suchlike, which show that gunpowder though epoch-making did not have the field entirely to itself. An examination of the staff and workers seems to indicate that they were interchangeable. We have seen that the ammunition of wooden and explosive artillery was common but the quarrels were going out of fashion. The records of the middle of the fourteenth century give many instances of cannon firing leaden projectiles.

The tail mentioned above shows that attempts had been made at elevation. But the first ideas of movable elevation were crude. A wedge or series of wedges was deemed sufficient to alter the angle of the bed, tiller, trunk or bedstock, whatever it might be called at the moment. The system of wedges or coigns was not a passing one and remained in use up to the end of the eighteenth century—which shows how man's inventive powers are limited on some occasions.

A French Royal decree of May 1375 referred to twenty-four cannons of copper. The average weight was about seventeen pounds, which indicates that they were small. In 1378 Richard II directed Thomas of Norwich to provide 'two greater and two lesser ingenia vocata canons'. These were to be sent to the Castle of Bristol. At the same time the King ordered 600 stones and materials for gunpowder. It is in an Issue Roll of the same reign that we find a gunner might be responsible for more than one gun. Payments were made to Sir Thomas Beauchamp, Captain of Carisbrook Castle, for five cannoniers each with his own cannon and for one cannonier with three cannon. Of course the latter might have had a weapon on the lines of an organ or a ribaudequin.

The Privy Wardrobe accounts show that Ralph de Halton, Keeper of the same, bought as many as seventy-three guns from William Woodward, gun-founder, between the years 1382 and 1388. Four of these were to be made of copper and between them they weighed 600 pounds. Fifty-two of them weighed over 318 pounds each and one as much as 665 pounds. This latter was an unusual type have a large central bore with ten smaller ones arranged around it. The central one threw stones and the other ones pellets or bolts. Double guns are also included in the accounts, showing how the inventor continually strove for the perfection of a new idea. One advantage of these cast cannon was that they did not suffer from weakness at the breech end, but the time taken to load must have been considerably more. The time element could have been little worry to the gunner who much preferred having a whole skin.

It may be mentioned here that for many years on the continent the credit of the first man to cast guns was given to a founder called Aarau of Augsburg, and the date is given as 1378. There are many references to guns found a quarter of a century before this time and so the claim does not appear very good. But the statement has been accepted and passed from book to book, even in modern times.

3. GIANT GUNS

One phenomenon that occurred in the fourteenth century was the giant cannon. The normal cannon having been well established in warfare, the metal workers strove for a super-weapon. Perhaps it was the iron-workers who feared the competition of the brass founders or perhaps it was the trial of strength between one rich lord and another. There were many specimens brought into being about the same period and one such effort which was made in Caen has been described in detail in contemporary accounts. On the 21st March 1375, three large forges began the work and five master forgers with their apprentices worked for forty-two days to complete the *bouche a feu* by the 3rd May. The itemized accounts give costs of all the raw materials, including the large wooden carriage. When finished the cannon was bound around with 90 pounds of rope and covered with an ox-hide to protect it against rain and rust. Four pulleys were necessary to handle it and raise the barrel to its wooden bed. The total metal employed weighed 2,364 pounds and the whole gun cost over £5,000, a vast sum for those days. Big though this may seem it was only a fraction of the weight of others which followed.

Farther north about the same time another giant cannon was constructed. Froissart says that in about 1382 Philippe van

Artevelle at the siege of Audenarde (Oudenarde) had a marvellously large bombard made, the mouth of which was 'cinquante trois pouces de bec' (53 inches) across. The noise of its discharge was such 'that one might suppose all the devils in hell were abroad', and it could be heard at the distance of five leagues by day and ten at night.

This appears to be the very bombard that is now in Ghent. Voison, writer of a guide to Ghent, says that it was most likely made when Philippe besieged Oudenarde in 1382. It is certain that the citizens of Ghent used it in 1411 and in an attack on Oudenarde in 1452. When they had to abandon the siege, the city took over the cannon and caused the arms of Burgundy to be engraved on it.

In 1578 the people of Ghent recaptured their cannon and later put it on a stone pedestal where it can be still seen. Eighteen feet long, the bombard now known as 'Duille Grete' has a mouth 2 feet 9 inches across and weighs 33,606 pounds. It threw a stone weighing 600 pounds. The barrel has thirty-two iron bars and over it are forty-one rings to bind it together. The chamber has twenty rings welded together.

In the same category is the 'Dardanelles' gun, still to be seen in the Tower of London near the Ravens' home. When Mohamet the Second besieged Constantinople in 1453 he engaged Urban, a Hungarian renegade, to make extra large cannon. In specially constructed gun-foundries at Adrianople, Urban and his fellow workers produced monster bronze siege guns. The 'Dardanelles' gun made then, 17 feet long and over 17 tons in weight, lay useless for many years overlooking the Dardanelles. The gun could have fired over this stretch of water if necessary for its range was nearly a mile. Its stone cannon balls according to a Turkish account weighed up to 1,200 pounds. In 1867 Sultan Abdul Aziz gave it to Queen Victoria. After resting at Woolwich until 1929 it was finally transferred to the Tower of London where it is on view to all.

The Arsenal at St. Petersburg also at one time had a large cannon 21 feet long but only weighing 17,435 pounds and carrying a shot of 68 pounds.

Yet another of these oversized cannon is in the British Isles. In Edinburgh on the Castle mound is the famous gun known as Mons Meg. This is constructed on the same principle as the

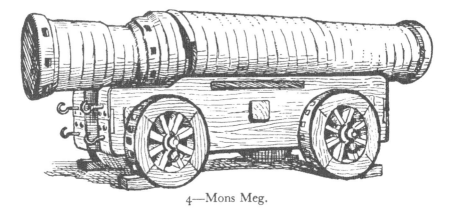

4—Mons Meg.

foregoing giant cannon, but exactly when and by whom is in doubt. The tradition is that when James the Second of Scotland and his army arrived at the Dee in 1451 to besiege Threave, the last stronghold of the Douglases, the M'Lellans presented him with this gun. Molise McKim, hereditary smith of Thrien, was supposed to have fashioned it at a temporary forge. As a reward the smith was given the estate of Mollance pronounced 'Mowans'. The gun, named after his loud-speaking wife, was called 'Mowans Meg', later 'Mons Meg'.

Sir Walter Scott, antiquarian as well as novelist, was satisfied with this story but others have criticized it, pointing out that Mons Meg was never its title in ancient days. In 1489 an account of the Lord High Treasurer of Scotland recorded eighteen shillings being paid for gunners' drink when they 'cartit Monss, by the King's Command'. 'Monss' is the name given in other accounts and it is not until 1650 that there appears a mention of 'the great Iron Murderer, called Muckle Meg' written by no less than the hand of Oliver Cromwell himself. It is a newspaper of 1660 that at last uses the expression 'Mounce Meg'. It is suggested that as Flanders was the main home of early cannon the name 'Mons' refers to the Town of Mons. We know that Scotland imported her cannon, for when James the Second in 1460 besieged the castle of Roxburgh he employed his 'new bombarde, lately cast in Flanders, called the Lion'. We also know that James the First of Scotland had a giant bombard cast for him in Flanders in 1430. This weighed 3,000 pounds and was called the 'Great Lion'. Whether this is meant for the same cannon, is not clear. But an interesting point arises, for in 1453 an iron bombard named 'Mons' was forged. It weighed 15,356 pounds, was 15 feet long, chamber and piece, and threw stones 18 inches in diameter weighing about 300 pounds. 'Mons Meg' is 13 feet 6 inches long, weighs 14,560 pounds according to Sibbald Scott, and has a calibre of 20 inches. There is not much difference in the two sets of measurements and one wonders if the same gun is not intended.

'Mons Meg' did not stay all the time in Scotland. It was fired off in 1682 in honour of a visit from the Duke of York (later to be King James the Second of England) and the ancient gun burst. This broken part can still be seen to the rear of the gun on the right side, and below the broken rings, one can see clearly the longitudinal strips of iron. When Mons Meg burst its barrel, it lay dismounted and neglected until 1753/4 when it was removed to the Tower of London because all unserviceable guns were to be returned to the store of the Board of Ordnance. It was not broken up but preserved, and later Sir Walter Scott made patriotic efforts to secure its return to Scotland. In 1829 George the Fourth ordered the cannon to be taken to Edinburgh. Pipers played before it on the last part of the journey when it was accompanied by the 73rd Regiment of Foot and three troops of cavalry. The cannon was placed on an ornamental carriage but in recent years was given a more appropriate one based on an old carving in the gateway of the Castle.

England also had these large cannons of which two still exist but unfortunately not in British hands. These are the two, preserved in the Castle of Mont St. Michel in Normandy, and are relics of a siege which began in 1423.

One gun is 12 feet long and 19 inches in diameter and the other is 11 feet 9 inches long with a 15-inch calibre. The largest weighs over 5 tons. The cannon balls now remaining are of various sizes; one of granite 18 inches in diameter weighs 300 pounds. As a token the Artillery Museum at Woolwich was given one of these shot. The smallest cannon has 'eyes' on the sides for rings to be attached, no doubt for easier handling.

All these giant guns seem to have been constructed in the same manner, as has already been described for chambered cannon. The red hot rings often 3½ inches wide were forced on the long bars and when they cooled they contracted, making a very tight fit. The rings varied in thickness, those at the breech end frequently being thicker. Whereas in the earlier and smaller types a few rings were sufficient, on these giants the lateral bars were completely covered. In smaller guns, the powder chamber was made removable for loading. On these large cannon, the charge chamber was also made separately but constructed with a large screw thread. Square holes were made at the sides and handspikes were used in these sockets to gain sufficient purchase to unscrew or screw the two pieces as necessary. Much effort and many men would be necessary for this difficult job. The suggestion that the rear piece was unscrewed every time the gun fired does not seem very practical, for the barrel would have to be unshipped from its bed and the rear part moved well away to be reloaded. To load through the muzzle seems to be the easiest method. The purpose of two pieces would appear to have been a lighter burden when travelling, and to allow simpler replacements if one part wore out or burst.

But the giant cannon were a passing fashion. They were not the weapon to end all war and their expense and awkwardness led to their disuse. Normal cannon, especially the cast varieties increased in popularity. Cast cannon were also attached to the wooden bed by means of rope, and rings were frequently attached to the barrel. One such type is in the Musée de l'Armée in Paris. This cast cannon came from Rhodes but had been made on the mainland, for an inscription in German reads—'My name is Catherine. Beware of my contents. I punish injustice. George Endorfer cast me. Sigismund, Archduke of Austria. Anno 1404.' It is 12 feet long with a diameter of 2 feet.

Cast cannon did not mean the end of chambered cannon. A curious invention came in the early fifteenth century which the Italians called a *bombardo cubito*. It was a development of the 'L'-shaped wooden bed but the barrel was placed nearly upright and the chamber or breech-piece was let into the side. An even later pattern had a short thick barrel placed upright on a platform with the small chamber let into the side. The platform had two small wheels and the whole could be moved forward or elevated by means of a shaft from the base-board. The fire from such an engine would be of an indirect nature but useful for firing over intervening obstacles in the manner of a mortar.

When Henry the Fifth decided to go on a warlike expedition to France, there was much activity in the way of preparation. Many of the original records relating to this occasion still remain in the Public Record Office and elsewhere. Among those listed in the roll taken before Agincourt in 1415 are four master gunners with others to the number of twenty-five, and each man had two servitour gunners, making a grand total of seventy-five.

Henry had many cannon made for him and the accounts of Gerard Sprong give details of the cannon which he made. Among the cast brass cannon was 'Foughler' weighing 11 hundredweight, one great cannon called the 'Kynges doghter' which broke at the siege of Hardelagh (Harlech), one other great cannon called 'le George' weighing over 36 hundredweight, one called 'Messager' over 44 hundredweight and 'Gobette' only of 11 hundredweight. There were also iron cannon with strange names, such as 'Godegrace', 'Joesue Nelpot', 'Clyff' who had two chambers, 'Neelpot' and 'Messager' both said to have been broken at the siege of Aberystwith. It would appear that when a gun exploded or broke, the name was transferred to another, much in the way that ships continue to use famous names throughout the centuries. Henry took with him to the siege of Harfleur cannon named 'Messager', the 'King's Daughter' and another called 'London'.

Shakespeare has made us familiar with the story of the Dauphin of France, who insulted Henry the Fifth by sending him a tunful of tennis balls, and of Henry's threat to send cannon-balls in return. John Lydgate at the time wrote a poem on the siege of Harfleur 1415 in which three cannons make the tennis strokes.

> 'Fyftene before' seyd London, tho
> His ball wol faire he gan it throwe,
> That the stepyll of Harflete and bellys also,
> With his breth he dide down blowe,
> 'XXXti is myn,' seyd Messagere,
> And smartly went his way
> Ther wallys that were mad right sure,
> He brast them down the sothe to say.

The Kynges doughter, seyde here, thei play
'Herkenyth myne maudenys in this tyde,
Fyve and forty that is no nay'
The wallys wente doun on every syde.

The scores of 15, 30 and 45 are said to refer respectively to the weight of the stones shot from the three cannon.

When Harfleur fell, Henry the Fifth marched on to engage the French army at the Battle of Agincourt. Apart from a reference by the defeated Maréchal de Boucicaut to several pieces of English cannon firing from an eminence, little evidence is forthcoming as to what might have been used in the field.

Ships at the same period were equipped with cannon. An ancient Roll under the date of 22nd June of the twelfth year of Henry the Fourth, or 1411—frequently misquoted as 1338—has details of ships' indentures. 'X'potre (Christopher) de la Toure' had 'iii canons de ferr ove V chambers' and a handgun. A further cannon of iron is mentioned with two chambers and another of brass with but one chamber is included in the inventory. 'Bernard de la Tour' had two iron cannon, one iron cannon with two chambers, another of brass and also a 'ketell'. Whether this last was an article of cooking or a type of mortar is not clear. The methods of mounting cannon aboard ship would be interesting, but no clue is given.

Henry had no conclusive result from his invasion of France and on his return to England made further preparations for a further invasion which took place in 1417. The 7,000 stone shots made by John Benet of Maidstone, a mason, for John Louthe, Clerk of the Ordnance, shows the type of projectile in use at the time. An account of 5th June 1416 of money paid to William Wodeward, founder, for the purchase and providing of cannon and gunpowder suggests cast cannon. An ancient manuscript speaks of 'tripgettis and engines' as well as 'gonnes' so the old wooden artillery was still used, no doubt with good effect on the walls of the fortesses later besieged.

A contemporary illustration of Caen which surrendered 4th September 1417 is in the 'Warwick Pageant'. Here 'Erle Richard' of Warwick is shown speaking to a gunner who kneels beside his cannon. The barrel appears to be about six feet long and is half embedded in its baseboard. The gunner holds the loose chamber above the breech and although this manuscript is said to have been made in about 1485 the cannon would not have been so very different. Other pictures in the same work show similar cannon, all with a projection at the top of the muzzle ring, possibly as an aid for sighting and laying the gun.

In the Tower of London is a breech-loading cannon (No. 19/4) of a similar type to those in the manuscript. Its barrel is 9 feet 6 inches long and the bore is 5½ inches across. The construction is still the old system of long bars held together by many iron hoops, the foremost of which, the muzzle ring, has a finial in the shape of a fleur-de-lis, also to be used for sighting. To aid lifting and possibly for fixing to the base are eight large rings, four on each side.

Another gun at the Rotunda, Woolwich, has a length of 7 feet 6 inches and calibre of 4½ inches; and since part of the breech-end has been broken away we can clearly see its construction. Fourteen long bars, two deep, arranged in a circle have the imperfections of the welding filled in with lead. A bronze cylinder serves to hold the powder for the breech end.

The limitations of propping the whole gun up by means of wedges were obvious and many ideas were tried before the invention of trunnions. One idea was to pivot the front edge of the chase or bed which held the barrel. One version had the main body built like a solid box; the front part of the bed was hinged and the rear part was adjusted in height by means of a cross bar of iron which went through the right pair of holes in two posts. The idea of temporarily fastening a gun-barrel to its bed was abandoned when casting improved and they became smaller. The practice of partly imbedding the metal needed only small straps over the top to complete the fixing. This method also led to the discontinuance of the breech-loader.

Early in the fifteenth century, there were sufficient numbers of cannon for them to be divided into categories. Unfortunately the names used in different parts of Europe were not the same although they might refer to a similar group. Colonel Fave who worked with Napoleon the Third on his famous work, classified them, with the bombards as the largest. These were often over 10,000 pounds in weight with the chamber-piece screwed on in action but removable for transportation.

The next largest group were the veuglaires, vöglers or fowlers which ranged from 10,000 down to 300 pounds in weight. These cannon were up to eight feet long and had removable chambers for breech-loading. Later they were distinguished by the strap which went around the loose piece and kept it attached to the main mass.

Next down the scale were 'crapaudeaux' which also had removable chambers but were only four to five feet long and with a diameter of two to four inches. The name 'toad' may have been given because of the squat appearance made by the gun when it rested low down on its wooden bed.

The next group was called 'couleuvres' or 'couleuvrines' meaning snakes or adders, and these guns were normally muzzle-loading. There is an even smaller group known as hand-couleuvrines, some of which weighed 30 pounds, but this last group really belongs to the musket section.

Most of these names were in use at much later dates when they came to mean different types rather than a division of weight. Mortars were also in use, as were ribaudequins, but these we deal with elsewhere. Later in the century a new name appears—that of 'serpentine' which indicated a firearm slightly larger than a couleuvrine. This is only natural for one expects serpents to be larger than snakes.

But there were many other ideas which did not fit into these groups, and the manuscript and later the printed books show many strange ideas, which look suspiciously as though they never got farther than the drawing stage.

A manuscript dedicated to the Emperor Sigismund in about 1430 has over 230 drawings of invention and items of warfare. One is a very low four-wheeled platform bearing a long cannon with a very wide mouth. This might be run up to a stout doorway to blow it down. Complicated and frail methods are shown of ways to elevate and turn gun-barrels in various directions. The more weird the idea the better the chance that it was repeated in the later printed works which appeared on these oddities right up to the seventeenth century.

But it was still the tiller or bed which permitted controlled elevation and it was not until the invention of trunnions by an unknown genius that the next step forward could be taken. The Archives of the town of Lille have an entry under the year

1465 for the making of a trunnion for a serpentine—a very early date for this innovation.

Having devised methods of laying or pointing a gun, the next stage for the inventor was to find a better means of mobility. Bringing a cannon up on a four-wheeled wagon and then assembling it on the spot was not the ideal method. Some cannons with the hinged beds were on solid square carriages that were made movable by four small wheels, but these were not suitable for long distance travelling. Two wheeled platforms with long shafts behind were also employed. Screens and mantelets were sometimes placed on the front of the platform.

Another variation was to place the barrel in a long trough. Two small but strong wheels were placed at the front for mobility while two sharp down-curving pieces at the rear made a grip on the earth to counteract the recoil. A treatise by Marianus Jacobus surnamed Taconole written in 1449 preserved in Venice shows this pattern which may have been in use earlier. The Swiss as early as 1443 had two-wheeled carriages for their cannon, known as *tarras-büchse*. The wheels are larger than those formerly used and are more akin to the size used on farm wagons. The simple frontlet or shield had now developed into a pent-roof like that of a dog-kennel, covering most of the barrel and protecting the gunners to some degree.

Previously artillery had been mainly used at sieges and in fortresses but now they could be used to advantage on the moving battlefield. They need not be deserted to a threatening enemy but could keep up with the infantry.

The expedition to France planned by Edward the Fourth in 1475, for all its careful thought to include such material as leathern boats and floating bridges, still had ordnance of the old type which had to be carried on wagons or chariots. Separate chariots were needed for a great iron gun, a great brazen gun, the chamber of the brazen gun plus a pot-gun of iron, an iron gun called the Messenger, a bombardell called the Edward, a fowler and her chamber called the Fowler of Chester, another fowler called Megge, another Fowler of the Tower, a Less Fowler of the Tower and two great pot-guns of brass. A mighty train but a cumbersome one.

On the Continent the exchange of military knowledge was much more rapid and such a great military leader as Charles the Bold of Burgundy was quick to see the advantage of wheeled artillery and use it in his wars against the Swiss. As usual the manuscripts illustrating these campaigns are made long after the events and so the details cannot be treated as contemporary evidence. But something much better remains and that is the actual cannon used in these battles. The Swiss troops captured many of these weapons from Charles the Bold and they are preserved in various museums. Cannons captured at Morat in 1476 are in the Musée de l'Armée, Paris and the 'Gymnasium' at Morat, while some captured at Grandson and Nancy in 1477 are in the Museums of Lausanne and Neuville.

Although at least one leading authority says the artillery of Charles the Bold had no trunnions, Colonel Fave illustrates two examples which he says were preserved until his days. Another cannon from the Isle of Rhodes inscribed 1478 and made for Louis the Eleventh has thick trunnions cast into the main mass. The Burgundian cannon all have strengthening rings at intervals. Some patterns are short, somewhat like mortars but firmly fixed into tillers or beds and hinged for elevation. The long slender cannon like the one preserved at Neuville, still retains the lifting rings on either side. As the barrel is fixed to its bed the whole upper part is pivoted to the trail, wheels and axle. The extent of the elevation or depression is regulated by two large arcs rising from the trail, between which the touch-hole end rises or falls.

Charles the Eighth of France took with him to the Kingdom of Naples large and medium couleuvrines as well as large and small falcons. Later these names came to indicate cannon with trunnions. A very small piece of Charles the Eighth's time in the Musée de l'Armée in Paris shows this new addition. It has an inscription in French which reads 'Given by Charles the Eighth to Bartemi, seigneur of Paris, captain of the bands of artillery in 1490.' The fore part of the cannon is eight-sided but the rear is rounded. There is a 'tail' for moving the piece up and down on the trunnions which run across the lower part of the barrel in one continuous bar.

Most valuable information comes from a series of manu-script books made for the Emperor Maximilian. These show

5—Cannon, early sixteenth century.

water-colour drawings, exquisitely finished of the cannons, the mortars and the other weapons in the arsenals of his various castles. These 'Zeugbuchs' were made by different artists in the early years of the sixteenth century.

Huge cannon fixed to wheelless beds bear the arms of Burgundy, showing that the old weapons of Charles the Bold were still in use. But most cannon are shown with wheels and trunnions for elevation. Many of the medium-sized guns have the new device of lifting handles. Curved bars of metal placed near the point of balance on the barrel were used for moving the metal piece from place to place. The simple loose rings placed on the sides were no longer in use, no doubt because of their weakness, and the new artifice had some unusual modes of expression. For example a cannon dated 1508 had the projecting knobs finish as dogs' heads. Another of 1535 used two human heads and others continued the idea of dogs. The fancies are shown in ancient French works but the German books show evidence of a more simple and practical nature— plain pieces sometimes bowing over to join at both ends. The invention remained in use until the middle of the nineteenth century.

The invention of trunnions meant that the barrel could rise upwards unless some method of fixing was applied. In some cases a wedge of wood between the end of the barrel and the carriage was sufficient; but in some pictures the presence of a square socket in the trail and a key or handle on the ground shows that some mechanical means may have been employed.

Two cannon on one carriage were used and to avoid weakness where the trunnions entered the carriage, they were staggered, one pair of trunnions placed forward and the other to the rear. Arising from this use of twin cannon, came the idea of using two shots connected with a chain. This would have covered a wider path of destruction but needed the precise action of both cannon going off at the same moment.

Another innovation which appears in the Zeugbuch was the use of an ammunition box on the trail or carriage. This is the beginning of an idea which lasted almost until modern times.

The advent of the manœuvrable cannon on two wheels also brought a limber with two wheels. It was not easy for horses to pull directly on a cannon as the down-drag of the trail would be too much for the pair of horses nearest the gun. The simple limber with an axle on a pair of wheels was sufficient to overcome this difficulty. A spike on the limber and a hole in the gun-trail was the device for connecting the two. This is another invention which remained in general use until the British found another method in the late eighteenth century. The wheeled cannon could now quite easily keep up with a marching army and efforts were made to achieve even more rapid means by the production of very light cannon. These were made with the trail split in two, giving shafts which allowed a single horse to draw the cannon.

4. HENRY THE EIGHTH'S INFLUENCE AND ELIZABETHAN CANNON

Gun barrels were now becoming the opportunity for craftsmen to display their art. The founders made long elegant shapes, some with fluted barrels like graceful architectural columns, others twisted like fantastic chimneys. Fanciful heads or beasts were incorporated into the cascabel or finial at the touch-hole end. Foliage and decoration appeared on the lifting handles and on the barrel. It was a graceful period and one of which many examples remain in this country.

The Tower of London and the Rotunda still have examples of Tudor gun barrels. Henry the Eighth was proud of his artillery and as early as the first year of his reign we find activities in that field. Although the price of tin—a material used in the bronze mixtures—had risen, the King made sure that he had enough supplies to have a hundred pieces of ordnance cast. Humphrey Walker was appointed Gunner at the Tower for life and the art of gunnery was to flourish. But the new cannon did not come quickly enough for Henry and so sources abroad were tapped. Hans Poppenruyter, Master Founder at Malines in Flanders in 1510, was to make forty-eight guns with appropriate names and badges. The Flemish master was given more work and made at least 140 guns of all types including a group known as the Twelve Apostles, which were later employed against Tournai and other towns. It is sad to relate that in 1513, the carters mistook their way and carelessly caused 'St. John the Evangelist' to be overthrown into a deep pond of water from which some time was needed to rescue him. The Emperor Charles the Fifth also had twelve guns cast which he named after the twelve Apostles. Louis the Twelfth had twelve brass guns of a great size also cast, but these he named after the twelve peers of France. The Spanish and the Portuguese named their guns after saints, other countries were not so respectful.

Henry the Eighth did very well with his collecting of artillery, in fact so much had he accumulated that the Venetian ambassador reported to the Doge that Henry had 'enough cannon to conquer Hell'. Another ambassador later reported that he saw at the Tower of London 400 examples of bronze artillery all mounted on their carriages. Henry encouraged the foundries in his own country. John and Robert Owen of Houndsditch produced guns which still exist. A Frenchman, Peter Baude, and the Italian family of Arcana were encouraged to make cannon in England and given citizenship papers.

The reproduction of the large wall-paintings made at Cowdray in Henry's reign show masses of long barrelled cannon arranged in batteries attacking the town of Boulogne in 1544. 'Carts of War' and heavy mortars were also employed on this occasion.

According to Holinshed's *Chronicles* the first iron cannon were cast in England at Buxted, then known as Buckesteed, in 1543 by Ralph Hoge and Peter Baude. This preparation for the coming battle was made with an eye to cheapness for iron did not cost as much as brass or bronze. They apparently were successful and demanded by people abroad for the King made restrictions on their export.

Information about the type of cannon used by the navy comes from the English ship the *Mary Rose* which sank off Spithead during an action with the French fleet on the 19th July 1545. This ship had many guns on board, several of which were rescued in 1836 by Anthony Dean who had invented a diving bell. Two of these are to be seen in the Tower of London, one of them over six feet in length. The style of manufacture is the old wrought iron variety with the shrunken rings. The breech of one still remains, with a stone shot in the barrel. The lifting rings on each side have not rusted away and even some of the oaken bed is preserved. Apart from these bar and hoop guns, there are brass guns rescued from the same ship, some 18-pounders and even larger—32-pounders. One of these brazen 'cannon royal' was made by John Owen and is beautifully decorated with roses and fleur-de-lis, while the lifting handles are made in the fashion of lions' heads.

There were experiments apart from the normal barrel and a Tower of London inventory of 1547 mentions 'Broad Fawcons shoting iij shotte'. Although damaged in the fire of 1831, a large bronze triple gun still remains to be seen in the crypt. 'Petrus Baude Gallus' was the maker according to the metal work. This fine piece has a rectangular breech with three compartments, one for each barrel. Peter Baude was paid £20 for making bronze ordnance in 1528—long before he went into iron founding at Buxted.

Two other Tower cannon are the bronze one from the 'Great Mary' dated 1542 which is 10 feet long with a calibre of 8.25 inches and a 'cannon of seven' dated 1548 and 12 feet 6 inches long. The crowned rose is a device used on English cannon at this date. Another bronze cannon made by 'John and Robert Owine, Brethern' was in 1549 sent to the Isle of Wight for the use of the local Militia. It weighed nearly two hundredweight and was 4 feet long. Valuable though it might be from the archaeological point of view, it was also considered valuable as scrap metal and was stolen in January 1954. Luckily it was recovered from a scrap-merchant later in the year.

There is a manuscript of 1552 in the Bibliothéque National.

Paris, which shows designs of artillery of Charles-Quint. This monarch possessed 520 pieces of artillery in at least fifty different patterns. Unfortunately only the barrels are depicted in this record but they tell us many facts. The drawings are based on actual examples stored at various centres. One dated 1494 on the metalwork has trunnions but another of 1506, a small cannon, has no trunnions. All the other cannon have trunnions so this innovation was firmly established. One small cannon is a breech-loader and has a movable box which is fixed in place by a small iron wedge. But the great majority were muzzle-loaders. It will be noted that obsolete cannon were always being used with the newest types. The need of economy was just as necessary in this field as it was in others, including armour where descendants wore their ancestors' armour altered to their needs.

Lifting handles had now become complete arcs and not studs or knobs. That did not prevent them from being made in fantastic shapes like mythological animals and fishes. The creature which attained the greatest popularity was the dolphin and it became so widespread that the very handles became known as dolphins.

An ancient manuscript quoted in Grose's *Military Antiquities* has the following information:

'Item, as a towne is wonne, whether it is by assalt, per force, subtile practice, or by anie other manner given up, be it towne, castell, pyle, church, or bastile, or fortresse, the chief master of the artillerie, or his lieutennent, shall ordayne, that the master gunners and their companie shall have the best bell within that place soe wonne, or the churchwardens shall appoint or compound with the great master of the artillerie and his counsell——.'

This right to church bells no doubt arose from the need of brass or bronze with which to cast new artillery. In France the Grand Master of the Artillery was permitted not only the church-bells but the kitchen utensils of copper and similar metal.

In Dover is a 23-foot long gun, popularly known as Queen Elizabeth's Pocket Pistol. Actually it was made at Utrecht in 1544 and given by the Emperor Charles the Fifth to Henry the Eighth. This gun is richly ornamented with groups emblematic of peace and war and on the breech is an elaborate inscription in Flemish which roughly translates as:

> *Over hill and dale I throw my ball,*
> *Breaker my name of mound and wall.*

There is a brass sakeret of Edward the Sixth's reign which is 6 feet long and has this inscription—'Thomas Owen made thys/pece for the Yel of/Garnce vhan Ser pete/r Meutes vas Governo/r and Captayn. Anno Dmi 1550.' Owen's Welsh accent comes through the ages on the gun made especially for the Isle of Guernsey. Thomas's brother John was unfortunately drowned at London Bridge but Thomas continued in business to become Gunfounder to Queen Elizabeth.

A return or check of stores and ordnance in the Tower of London and on the ships made in 1578 showed that there were 104 different guns in the former place and 504 brass ordnance actually aboard ships. The ships' artillery included cannon pieces, demi-cannon, culverings, demi-culverings, sakers, minions, fawcons, fawconets and fowlers arranged in the order of their size.

Artillery had now achieved most of the developments necessary to perform the functions needed in warfare. The muzzle-loader was the accepted piece, although the breech-loader still retained a small 'claim in the fowler. The method of founding remained static for the same period and in fact little was done except make refinements and compile statistics. Books on gunnery appeared and the sizes of the length and bores were standardized. It is claimed that the word ordnance comes from the laws or ordinances passed to regulate the dimensions. Range tables were worked out and gunnery became a science with quadrants and instruments, to say nothing of elaborate calculations and theories.

The old books which were supposed to deal with the art of war were now succeeded by practical works. The ancient writers seemed to have been more concerned with the curiosities and included such amazing inventions as an Arabic machine. This took the form of a gigantic wickerwork dragon which sat upright on a wheeled platform. There was a kind of portcullis in its chest to come into action when it came to a wall. Cannons appeared all over its body and its crown was made of spears. This monstrosity was to be pulled forward by means of ropes and pulleys fixed near the enemy. However it or its operators would last a moment in serious warfare is hard to see. Then there was the turntable with cannon all around the edge and this was operated by a remote-control wheel. Other items not within the scope of this work but mentioned to show the mind of these writers, included a soldier enveloped in a leathern suit walking under water with his shield on his arm ready to attack any straying enemy.

But to return to more serious matters. There is one distinct trend of development not yet mentioned—the pierrers, peteras, pattereras, from the root of 'stone'. These were the descendants of the old veuglairs or fowlers with removable chambers. Examples are in the Tower of London and Castel San Angelo, Rome. They were not large weapons and took a small stone ball. The chamber, fashioned like a pint-pot, is kept in place by means of a bar of metal slotted through the breech end. The mounting is usually a 'U'-shaped fork to take the trunnions the shaft of which could be placed in a wall or bulwark of a ship. They were pointed by means of the long tail at the breech-end. Popular though they were in Elizabethan times, they remained in use as a ships weapon in the seventeenth century and gradually died out during the next. A book of gunnery published in London 1628 describes 'port-peccys and fowlers' as typical naval ordnance. These are described in the book as being brass cast pieces open at both ends, loaded with chambers at the breech-end fitting with a shouldering.

There is a brass gun in the Tower made by Richard Phillips in 1601 which had a curious history. It somehow found its way to Cochin China where the Chinese captured it. In turn it was recaptured by the British at Chusan in 1842 and finally returned to its home.

5. THE SEVENTEENTH CENTURY

In 1620 a report was made on the brass ordnance in the Tower which included 'cannon of 7 and 12, cannon perriers, demi-cannon, culverins, demi-culverins, sakers, minions, faucons, fauconetts, portpieces with chambers, fowlers with chambers, robinets, mortar pieces and one bombard.' The iron ordnance covered a much smaller range including culverins, demi-culverins, sakers and one each of minions and faucon. It was from this collection that twenty pieces of artillery were selected to go on a more or less unofficial expedition for the recovery of the Palatinate. But the English did not have any major reason for employing their artillery in the reigns of James the First or Charles the First before 1639. Most of the military leaders gained their experience abroad and in small campaigns and the storehouse of cannon was not very important when the Civil War broke out. There was at this time a change from the employment of the large artillery and Gustavus Adolphus in his Thirty Years War employed the leather cannon and restricted his metal ones to nothing larger than a twelve-pounder. The English seemed to favour these limitations but whether by choice or necessity is not clear.

The few types favoured for field work included the culverin with a ball of 16 pounds, the demi-culverin with a ball of 9 pounds, the saker and drake with a ball of 5 pounds, the minion with a ball of 3½ pounds and the falcon with a 2½-pound shot.

There was a brass demi-culverin which King Charles had made in 1638 which was called simply 'The Gun', and placed in St. James's Park for the wondering Londoners to admire. The founder John Brown ornamented it with a crown, anchor and rose, a trident and staff. There was also an inscription which read 'Carolus Edgari sceptrum stabilivit aquarum', an allusion to Edgar who was the first Saxon King to establish a fleet capable of keeping these shores free from the Danes, which caused him sometimes to be called the founder of the British Navy. A brass fawcon of the same period, less than four feet long is at Woolwich. It will be noticed that the spelling constantly altered with the passing years and no doubt with the whim of the writer.

Proof that mainly small guns were in use is to be found in a contemporary newspaper account of the ordnance captured in June 1644 by the Royalists. The list included '5 sakers, 1 Twelve pound Peece, 1 Demi Culverin, 2 Mynions, 2 three pound Peeces etc., besides two Blinders for Muskets and Leather Guns——.' Essex when defeated in Cornwall in

September 1644 allowed '49 pieces of fair brass ordnance' to be captured by the Royalists, including 'the great Basilisco of Dover'. This latter has been identified as the gun called 'Queen Elizabeth's Pocket Pistol'. Some of the guns were recaptured later. In fact the artillery was frequently changing hands for one reason and another. The lack of harness was the reason given when Rupert caused several large iron guns to be thrown into the Thames. It may be that they were not sufficiently mobile and under water he hoped for them to be well away from the Roundheads' clutches.

When Cromwell went to Scotland in 1650 he took with him the 'Twelve Apostles' in which he put his trust according to a statement of the time. When he captured Edinburgh Castle the same year he listed among the captured ordnance, not only 'the great murderer called Muckle Meg' but also several 'drakes called monkeys'.

Earlier in the Civil War the King, who had to make his headquarters at Oxford, kept his artillery behind Magdalen College. The train of artillery when it went forth to battle varied in size according to the task in hand. In 1647 a train from Oxford to St. Albans had sixteen culverins, ten sakers, fifteen drakes and fifteen small field pieces.

The old practice of giving names to cannon had not been discontinued for 'a list of what was taken at Newark' in 1646 included a 'Great piece of Ordnance called "Sweet-lips".' Generally speaking only small pieces were used and they did not always have a place in the plan of battle; so little were they appreciated by the leaders at the time.

As the people of England were not too sure about the Restoration of the Monarchy, Charles the Second was not permitted a standing army and the artillery men were dispersed in garrisons and old forts, only to be called together in a war. Thus little opportunity occurred for progress in the science of artillery. We hear of a brass falcon just over three feet long being cast with Charles's Royal Coat of Arms and a return of stores in the Tower 1669 mentions a brass piece of 'seven bores'. Although it is still in the inventory of 1690, it did not appear to be worthy of repetition.

James the Second had more immediate need for artillery. The rebellion of Monmouth and coming of William the Third gave

6—Cannon, early seventeenth century.

him much thought in military matters. The first trouble saw a train of artillery being raised with sixteen brass pieces, and another with eight pieces (four iron and four brass) from Portsmouth. The warrants for the raising of these trains are still in existence and they are full of details, even down to needles and bottles of ink. The artillery arrived in time to do its duty at Sedgemoor but it needed the assistance of the carriage horses and traces of the Bishop of Winchester (an old soldier) to get the guns into place. Even when in position the dearth of skilled gunners was felt; Sergeant Weems of Dumbarton's Regiment, now the Royal Scots, helped to lay several pieces and for such services received £40.

James's next train melted away before William's army which was equipped with wagons loaded with tin boats to make an artificial bridge. But no striking developments took part. The old names of pieces based on birds and animals were gradually giving way to names which described the weight of the shot, and the howitzer was a weapon increasing in popularity. Mortars were employed to make an indirect fire to clear intervening obstacles. Field pieces fired more or less directly. Howitzers came in between. Having a carriage like a field piece they could keep up with the normal army, and having a wide bore could fire shells and bombs like mortars but with more precision.

One English howitzer of which details are available was captured at the Battle of Neerwinden in 1693 when England fought with the Dutch against the French. The bronze barrel was over a yard long and the carriage, made as strong as those for cannon, was strengthened by iron bands and straps. It is

46

interesting to note that although the iron tyres were well studded, the felloes were not banded all round as was the practice in Continental cannon.

6. SLOW DEVELOPMENT

As mentioned before artillery remained for many years without any great change, not because no one tried but because of the lack of success. In fact a Frenchman, the Chevalier le Folard, was so disgusted with the failure of his careful experiments that he decided artillery as then known was incapable of further improvement and advocated a return to the ancient catapults.

The French had again brought out cannon with three barrels and in 1705 Marlborough's men captured eight pieces of this kind. Two of these taken at Malplaquet are at Woolwich, made at Douay in 1704 and 1706. The Tower of London has two specimens from about ten years earlier.

Although little progress had been made in the field artillery in the eighteenth century, progress had been made with garrison and ships' guns, although mainly in the carriages. For years ships had been made on solid low beds, for the restrictions of space below decks imposed these limitations. The recoil of guns was taken up by rope, blocks and tackle from iron rings in the carriages to the solid wooden walls of the ship. To load the guns, the ropes had to be slackened and run back. Strange to say all the difficulties of muzzle-loading did not inspire anyone in the Navy to produce a breech-loader. Even the introduction of a special carriage and a shortened barrel had to wait for the ingenuity of the Carron factory.

Fortress guns were made on elaborate carriages. The actual barrel was mounted on the usual solid framework with small wheels. These in turn were placed on a short length of railway so that they could be run back for reloading or to take up the recoil. Then the whole of the 'railway' was slightly elevated and pivoted at the front and wheeled at the rear end so that it could manœuvre on an arc. Thus the gun could be pointed over a wide traverse.

An idea for improving cannon was thought of by a Colonel

Ludwig Wiedemann from Saxony in Germany. He induced William Duke of Cumberland in 1748 to try his new method at the New Foundry in Chelsea near the World's End Passage. A proposal was made to try these against those made by Mr. Schalch the official Master Gun-founder. So in April 1749 cannon were taken to Windsor Park where many high officers attended to see the results. Twenty-four, twelve and six-pounders were used by both founders and although the government founder fired all his rounds and hit the targets, the German not only scored no hits but failed to complete his rounds as a six-pounder burst. Obviously the new process could not be taken up but out of respect to the Duke of Cumberland the guns were purchased by the Ordnance and sent to the Tower as a souvenir of the occasion. Three of these have found their way to Woolwich where they are still preserved. Their defect is very plain, as was discovered when there was thought of melting them down in 1773. They were then noted as 'being made of lead covered with brass'. Observation shows that the brass contains much zinc. Some of Wiedemann's guns are also preserved in Copenhagen but here is a pioneer who trod a path which led nowhere.

Experimental guns were forgotten and production reverted to normal types produced by such fine craftsmen as J. Fuller of Heathfield, Sussex. His work was of such a high standard that he was proud to place his initials J.F. on the trunnions; a distinction which much to his annoyance was copied by inferior workmen.

In France an attempt had been made to improve their system of artillery. In October 1732 the King approved the measure taken by father and son Valliere. In theory it had been improved but the Vallieres were more courtiers than practical men. Gribeauval was the man who was destined to get results. Although he returned from Germany after commanding Austrian artillery he was not given a chance to show his genius until Valliere died in 1776. Gribeauval standardized the parts and generally polished up the production which remained in use until the wars of Napoleon. The garrison guns were separated from the field artillery but practically speaking there was no introduction or invention which altered any principle of gunnery, and England did not adopt the system.

The making of gun barrels was an elaborate system. The moulds were made with great care. Old ships' masts were frequently used as spindles. Normally in England guns were cast on an inner core but on the Continent they were cast solid and then bored out afterwards. In 1770 the British government obtained from Holland a replacement for the official gun founder. Very soon the Woolwich foundry was casting iron guns after the Swedish manner. In 1773 King George the Third made an impressive visit to the foundry in the Warren where he saw the new foundry, the processes of casting brass guns, the horizontal boring machine and other interesting objects. So successful was the visit that a Saturday in July was kept as a holiday up to recent times.

When the Sussex gun-foundries closed down one by one, their business went to Scotland. At Carron near Falkirk, Dr. John Roebuck with the Cadell family in 1759 began a factory. The metal for making the guns came mainly from the scrap of broken or captured guns at Woolwich. But the standard of work was so high that Wellington requested their work by name.

One of the difficulties of handling guns was that between decks the long barrel needed complicated handling and loading. It would appear that General Melville and Mr. Gascoigne, manager of the works, both helped to produce the short cannon known as the Carronade which had a hinge below instead of trunnions. The shorter and thus lighter gun was easier to handle and fired a shot which, having the full weight of a solid shot, could also carry inflammable material. The carronade was such a success that Gascoigne left the company in 1779, and went to Russia where he received the amazing salary of £4,500 per annum for creating cannon factories. By the end of his career he was a General in the Russian army and Counsellor to the Empress Catherine.

The elevation of a gun barrel for many generations had been accomplished by the simple means of inserting a wooden wedge shaped like a segment of cheese between the rear and lower part of the barrel and the trail. To increase the depression the wedge, coign or quoin was knocked in a little more and if this was not sufficient a second wedge was added. Care had to be taken that the barrel was not depressed below the

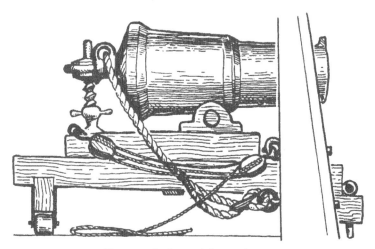

7—Carronade, late eighteenth century.

horizontal, otherwise extra wads would be necessary to stop the round shot from rolling out.

About 1780 a refinement was being added to the wedge. A horizontal screw ran through the quoin and forced it either in or out when it was turned. But by 1790 a better method was being employed. This was a capstan-headed screw mechanism fixed to the central transom of the trail. A long screw through the trail and going below the barrel was made turnable by means of a movable plate. Thus the barrel rose or fell by direct action. But the heavier eighteen and twenty-four-pounder guns retained the old wooden wedge well into the nineteenth century. In the fifteenth century a German manuscript depicted a gun not only elevated by a vertical screw but operating laterally by another long screw placed horizontally through the trail. It is a pity that such an idea did not develop, but remained lost until modern times.

A very advanced gun was the one-pounder produced by Dr. James Lind and Captain Alexander Blair. A book written by Lind in 1776 gives details of this weapon which weighed about a hundredweight. It was rifled with six channels semi-circular in section, which made one complete turn in the length of the barrel. The special lead projectile was spherical but had six studs cast on it so as to engage with the rifling. This gun was also designed with a telescopic sight. Unfortunately the gun, like other inventions, was in advance of its time and was not taken seriously. But most of its ideas were used later with success.

Documentation of the Royal Gun Factory from 1789 to 1803 shows that rifled cannon were being considered. Joseph Manton, a well-known gunsmith, desired to take out a patent in 1790 for a rifling machine and an improved shot with a base of soft wood to take the rifling. The Government refused to let him do so. Thus when the Duke of Richmond, interested in the development of horse artillery, invited Manton to lend rifled guns for trials, the gunsmith replied in no uncertain terms. However the Government made trials of wooden cups, which were blocks of soft wood slightly hollowed to take the cannon ball. The softness of the wood made a tight fit and acted as a gas-check. One of Manton's guns, a six-pounder, is in the Rotunda. It is made of brass and has sixteen grooves.

Trials were made in October 1792 at Goodwood, the seat of the Duke of Richmond, then the Master General of the Ordnance, between 'Rifled and Plane Medium 6 prs.' The rifled gun made a slightly better performance. The rifled gun was a bronze one by Manton but it did not have the success it warranted as it was not realized at that time that spherical ammunition was not satisfactory. The elongated projectile would have given much better results. It was the Duke of Richmond who introduced horse artillery into the British Army with gunners and drivers all mounted. The guns could keep up with cavalry and yet be ready for action in a matter of moments. The Duke was so proud of his innovation that he had the first troop move to his home at Goodwood where they lived in the stables and parked the guns in front of his house.

A distinct improvement introduced by the British was the block trail. For many years past, the flasque or cheeked open trail had been in use, but the great proportion of wood made a cumbersome carriage. It remained for the British at the end of the eighteenth century to introduce the improvement. Sir Howard Douglas had stated that he saw the original drawings for the block trail in Sir William Congreve's office. The first guns to be fitted were three-pounders and Sir William personally superintended the experiment and saw them brought into regular use in about 1790. The Horse Artillery was the first unit to adopt them, the rest not changing until much later.

After the Goodwood trial of 1792 rifled cannon lapsed, although from 1815 onwards proposals were being made for their use. In France H. C. Paixhans pointed out in 1835 that it was necessary to introduce rifled cannon, as the normal cannon would take a place of secondary importance to rifled small arms. This inventor did much in the field of gunnery and later produced a howitzer cannon.

By the 1840s the rifling of cannon was attaining some measure of success. Both Sardinia and Germany independently produced rifled cannons of iron in 1846, Major Cavalli in the former country and the Swedish Baron Wahrendorff in the latter. Both were also breech-loading. The Italian 6½-inch calibre gun had two grooves which made the projectile take a partial turn before leaving the barrel. Both these guns were tested at Shoeburyness but as the breech mechanism was deemed defective, neither was adopted. When the Crimean War began the English forces used rifled cannon which had been made by taking cast-iron smooth bore guns and adding rifling, on the Lancaster principle of the oval bore which had also been tried in small arms. Although the bombardment of Sevastapol was successfully accomplished with the aid of these cannon, the type did not continue in regular use. The oval bore was, of course, made with a twist and used for guns firing up to 68-pound projectiles.

7. MODERN METHODS

A radical change was now on its way, from cast guns to wrought iron. The process was slow but in May 1856 Messrs. Horsfall of Liverpool made a gun on the new principle which was 15 feet 10 inches long, weighing nearly 22 tons and firing a shot 2,000 yards. The cost was £3,000 and the gun was still muzzle-loading. The new method of manufacture was accepted and the next stage was to find a satisfactory method of breech-loading.

In 1854 a Tyneside civil engineer, William G. Armstrong, conceived a method of producing artillery by the wrought iron method. He was engaged by the Government for twelve years to carry on this work. In July of the next year he produced his first gun, part of an order of six. His method of construction was very similar to that used in the first cannon. He used a central gun but added hoops and layers to give extra strength where needed. This 'built-up' method was used by other nations quite successfully. On the 20th August 1858 a committee was appointed to study rifled ordnance and the next year Armstrong produced a wrought iron gun which was not only rifled but breech-loading, and had a range up to five miles. He was knighted in February 1859 and appointed Engineer-in-Chief of Rifled Ordnance.

By now rifled cannon were being made in various calibres, twenty, twelve, nine and six-pounders. The heaviest were used in Canada and the lightest went to the colonies. The projectiles were now oblong, a shape necessary to get the best results in the rifled barrels.

Although in August 1860 Armstrong guns were effectively used in attacks on the Taku Forts in China, a select committee appointed that year to report on ordnance commented unfavourably on the breech-loading system. Experiments continued and in 1862 solid shells pierced $5\frac{1}{2}$-inch iron plates and entered the wood placed behind. But Sir William Armstrong was not pleased with these trends and on 1863 resigned his appointment. In April 1864, competitions were held between the Armstrong and the Whitworth guns. Eventually it was decided that the breech-loading idea was all wrong. On the Continent the Prussian 9-inch breech loaders were being used with great success but Great Britain decided to return to ancient times and ideas. Thus muzzle-loading cannon were kept in use up to 1886.

Colonel Moncreiff in 1872 produced his ideas for a hydro-pneumatic carriage which absorbed the shock of the recoil. Armstrong was now producing larger and larger guns. A 100-ton gun was used at Spezzia in Italy which threw a 2,000-pound shot. Two years later the British Government ordered four guns of this calibre.

But Krupps had been conquering Europe with breech-loading guns, even producing them up to 130 tons for Italy. It was slowly realized that progress could not be ignored and in December 1879 breech-loaders were ordered. By 1885 it had to be conceded that rifled muzzle-loaders were out of date and in future field artillery was issued with breech-loaders.

8—Thirteen-pounder, twentieth century.

Artillery had now entered its stages of development as used in the First World War. The Krupps breech was in the form of a sliding block which entered the square breech traversely, but the British system had a hinged breech-plug which engaged by means of ingenious half threads and a half turn. The principle of a buffer and recuperator eased the recoil shock. A piston attached to the barrel or piece was connected with a cylinder and by means of springs, water or oil, slowed down the backward movement. A shoe to fit between the wheel and the ground also acted as a brake, as did the spade-recoil fitted below the carriage. The spade-recoil was also connected to a cylinder which acted on the buffer principle. The rapid improvement of instruments for sighting and laying guns, the disappearance of the wooden carriage and the changes in the pattern of the projectiles cannot be dealt with here. Garrison pieces, guns on railway mounting, anti-aircraft carriages, heavy howitzers and mountain guns could each have a chapter of their own, so complex is modern artillery. They must be left for another and much larger work.

III

VARIATIONS OF CANNON

~~~~~~

I. MORTARS

WHEN the first artillery developed, it was found that small projectiles could be fired more or less directly at the target. But heavier projectiles reacted to the pressure of air and dropped to the ground short of the mark. By increasing the angle of the gun it was found that heavy cannon-balls could be used but the path taken was an indirect one—a parabola. This led to the use of another type of gun, the mortar. This new trend of development led to short barrels, thicker walls to withstand the shock of exploding gunpowder, and wider bores or calibres. The wider mouth also permitted new types of projectiles to be used, such as balls and bar, and hollow shells filled with explosive mixtures which by means of a fuze went off in the air or on reaching the target. The mortar was useful in sieges because if a bombard could not batter its way through a wall or a gate, it could lob an explosive shell over the high wall and on to a powder store or some other vulnerable place.

It is said that mortars took their shape from the chemist's mortar which was used by 'Father Schwartz', but some authorities point out that marble slabs were used for mixing chemicals and that a chemists' mortar would have no strength at all. Also it is pointed out that the first bombards were open at both ends, making a hollow tube quite unlike any mortar. It appears that when the mortars came in use, they took their shape from objects already in use like the vases and *pots à feu* which had been employed for many years by the Arabs for pyrotechnical displays. In actual warfare these vases were of assorted shapes and filled with incendiary material. The vases were frequently pierced with holes and when flung by wooden artillery had the reputation of being noisome and fear-making. The Italians sometimes called them bombards but as they applied the word equally to pot, cannon or wooden engine, it meant little in the way of distinction unless it was an acknowledgement that the vase had become akin to a mortar.

The mortar was of one piece and had to be muzzle-loading, ignited by means of a touch-hole at the base. The projectiles used in the early days were metal arrows, lead balls, and even stone shot—all used once with wooden artillery but now pressed into service in the new field of discovery.

The weapon was named *mortarium* in Latin, but in Germany was known variously as *Moerser*, *Boeller*, *Böhler* or *Roller*. The latter words describe the bowling or rolling action of the cannon ball. The last word explains the presence of '5 Roleres' stored in the Guildhall of London in the reign of Edward the Third.

Around 1420 mortars were made with long tails or handles and fixed to low wooden trolleys. From the same period a very large mortar made at Stier in Austria is preserved in Vienna. It is of the forged circle-and-bar type, nearly 8 feet long and 3 feet 6 inches in diameter. It was captured by the Turks but regained by the Austrians in 1529. It is said that when the very large cannon were made in two pieces, the breech part was on occasion used as a kind of mortar.

In the moat of Bodiam Castle, Sussex, was found an early bombard in mortar shape. For many years it was preserved in Battle Abbey but in the nineteenth century it was sold to the Woolwich Rotunda. This may be the one called the Crécy Bombard without much reason or evidence. It is made like a large drum, over 15 inches across and 22 inches deep, but measuring 4 feet over all when one includes the 'tail' with the two fixing rings. The construction is by forged bands of wrought iron. The carriage is modern and useless as evidence.

It is said that the English at the siege of Orleans in 1428 used fifteen mortars loaded at the breech, but how they were operated is not made clear.

A stone mortar called *steinmörser* or *stein böhler* used at the siege of Waldeshut in 1468 is a simple tube placed nearly upright in a wood box, and of course it threw large stone cannon balls.

By 1470 the mortars appear to have followed the development of cannons and acquired trunnions. A British Museum manuscript of about 1480 shows one suspended between two uprights. The painting of the metal barrel seems to indicate the old bar-and-ring system of forging still in use. In the Ambrosian Library at Milan is a letter from Leonardo da Vinci, written to Ludovico il Moro, Regent of Milan, referring to a kind of portable bombard, capable of throwing hailshot. Sketches of bombs and shells were also included.

The Arsenals of the Emperor Maximilian contained many large mortars, which are of the cast variety and included much ornamentation and heraldry on their surface. They are shown with trunnions for laying the piece, and the wooden framework for holding them are of many fashions. A few have the side rings and many have at the base a large flat surface slightly curved which permitted the piece to be tilted to the necessary angle. Wooden wedges were driven beneath to prevent further movement. These *haubt morsers* had curious names such as 'Storch' (stork), 'Schwalb' (swallow), and 'Brachvogel' (curlew), all indicating the flying nature of the projectile.

The English took up the manufacture of mortars in 1543 when the Frenchman Peter Baude and one Peter van Collen were encouraged to produce them in England. Henry the Eighth got them to design mortar-pieces with a diameter of from eleven to nineteen inches. These were to project hollow shot 'stuffed with fireworks, or wild fire'. These shells had 'screws of iron to receive a match to carry fire kindled.' The wall-paintings at Cowdray, mentioned before, show a row of mortars casting their deadly burden at Boulogne. Proof is also given of the use of shells, for here too can be seen a workman wielding a mallet to drive in a fuze of a shell which rests on a three-legged table.

Science was now being used to make the path of the projectile more controlled than random, and a gunnery book of the sixteenth century shows a mortar with a quadrant and plumbline in its mouth. This particular mortar has the addition of four small but solid wheels; although not very mobile, it could keep up with a marching army.

The Commonwealth forces needed mortars and in 1657 a contract was made with Henry Quintyn to supply and to cast mortar pieces, at Snodland in Kent. They varied from 18½ inches to just over 12, and were to bear the arms of the Commonwealth and Cromwell. They were tried out at Millale near Aylesford on the Medway.

There was very little that could be done in the designing of mortars. Although the bore at the top was wide, a narrow section at the base served as the reservoir for the gunpowder —a plan which was practically constant through the ages. But the position of the trunnions varied. Early mortars had the trunnions placed towards the middle, but by the eighteenth century it was more common to place the trunnions right at the base. One of the most popular types was the Coehorn, named after Baron van Menno Coehorn, a Dutch engineer who used his pattern against the French in 1673 in a most effective manner. A peculiar distortion of the name was employed by the Spaniards who called them *cuernos de vaca*, cow-horn, their translation of his name. The British continued to use the Coehorns successfully in the Americas.

Normally mortars were of brass, bronze and gun-metal but iron might be used as in the Schulemburg mortars. Count Matthias Schulemberg who fought under the Pole John Sobieski had his own idea of what should be done, and produced an iron mortar combined with a cast-iron bed. From the example preserved in the Tower of London, one can see the distinctive feature of the turned-down front edge of the bed. As Schulemberg entered the service of the Venetians in 1711 many of his 'perriers' have upon them the device of the Venetian Lion.

Improvised mortars were made by the Polish soldiers in 1659 when they were besieging the Swedes in the town of Thorn in Prussia. Holes were dug in the ground at the correct angle. These were filled with gun-powder and broken millstones weighing anything up to 800 pounds. When ignited by means of threads dipped in spirits these elementary mortars did effective work.

Another improvised and successful method was employed

by Lieutenant Healy of the Royal Artillery at Gibraltar in 1771 when he conceived the idea of using the living rock. Holes were drilled into the rock at the proper angle, making a cavity 3 feet across and 4 feet deep. The shape was parabolic conoidial or as a contemporary writer says, in simpler words—shaped like a wineglass. The resulting volume of some fourteen cubic feet was filled with gunpowder, a wooden tompion and masses of small stones. The problem was ignition, but a hollow copper tube was placed in the centre through the stones and wood down to the powder. The powder inside took five minutes to burn before successfully flinging the stones into the near-by water. Ignited as it was centrally, it was deemed to have made a better explosion that if it had been set off from one side. The same 'mortar' stood up to further discharges without suffering. The difficulty was that the target must present itself to the correct position.

An even more unorthodox method was said to have been employed by the Russians in the mid-eighteenth century. They hollowed mortars out of ice and discharged ice cannon balls without danger to the gunners.

But generally mortars settled down to the pattern as shown in Diderot's *Encyclopedie*, with the trunnions placed at the base somewhat like a stout bar. The practice of ornamenting the brass pieces with mottoes, cyphers, dolphins and other devices make these articles of artillery into fine examples of the founder's art. Mortars were not mobile in the same fashion as normal cannon. The beds for mortars were made with lifting-rings and transported on wagons. The angle of some mortars was regulated by means of a hinged rod from the base to the barrel but in many cases they were cast at the fixed angle of 45 degrees.

Many miniature mortars exist and were used as signal or saluting guns, chiefly at the Tower of London. The artillery fired blank shots, and the Tower Warders added their quota by means of chamber pieces similar to those used in the ancient fowlers or veuglaires. In the nineteenth century they were also fired in the park on grand occasions and gave forth the same fine sound as heavy ordnance.

But mortars were beginning to go out of fashion. They were still being carefully studied and drawn at the Royal Military

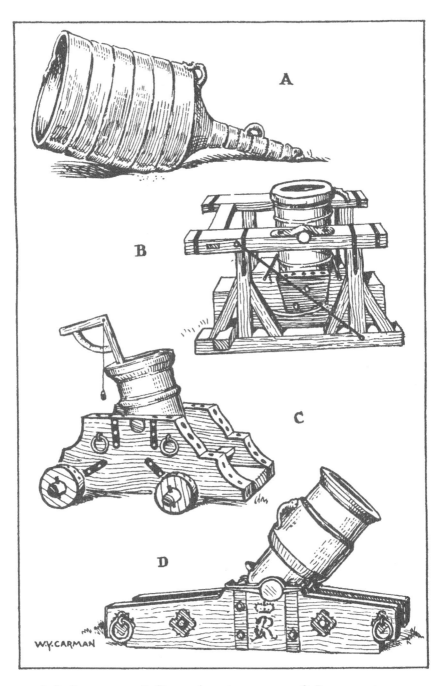

9—A. Bodiam mortar. B. Sixteenth-century mortar. C. Seventeenth-century
mortar. D. Eighteenth-century mortar.

Academy, and one made in 1788 for Spain was known as 'El Espanto', the Terror. This also had the fixed angle, and varied its range by the quantity of the charge. Battles were becoming more mobile and the mortar was not needed.

A comeback was made in the middle of the nineteenth century. A special mortar was designed in 1857. This was a giant affair which weighed 42 tons, had a calibre of 36 inches and could fire a shell weighing up to 3,000 pounds. The inventor, R. Mallet, constructed the monster on new principles and although the result was higher than a man, it was never used in action and never repeated. It can still be seen at Woolwich Arsenal. In appearance it is more like a futuristic concrete mixer than a weapon of war.

The American Civil War produced opportunities for mortars and the Federal Artillery employed a huge 13-ton mortar of cast-iron called the 'Dictator' in the bombardment of Petersburg, Virginia. But for long ranges, mortars were highly inaccurate and lapsed in use.

The fixed trench warfare of the First World War again brought the mortar into use but in a new form. The pattern was now little more than a simple tube into which an already 'fixed' or primed mortar shell was dropped. As it struck the base of the tube, the fuze was ignited and it immediately leapt out again. By such means a high rate of fire could be maintained. Accuracy was not a strong point but a barrage of such mortars could pin down an opposing party of men.

2. LEATHER GUNS

A popular curiosity which appeared in the seventeenth century was the 'leather' gun. Not only was it used on the Continent but also in the English Civil War, as an account of Ordnance captured by the Royalists, shows. The orthodox cannon are listed and then we notice 'two Blinders for muskets and Leather guns invented by Col. Weems, a Scot, who lately made them at Lambeth (in the same place where the Gun-Powder traytors practiced) and received 2000 L for them as appears by writing in his pocket.'

These leather guns were a fashion of the moment and the

credit of their invention is claimed for many persons. Indeed there is in Lambeth Church a monument to Robert Scott who died in 1631. The monument tells us that this Scotsman 'bent himself to travell and studie much, and amongst many other things, he invented the leather ordnance and carried to the Kinge of Sweden 200 men, who, after ten years service for his worth and valour was p'ferred to the office of Quarter Mr. General of His Matie Army.' When he went to Denmark he became General of the Artillery there.

The Weems or Wemyss mentioned above was the nephew of Robert Scott, which explains the Lambeth connexion, and he may even have helped to write the epitaph. Whether Wemyss made any improvement on Scott's invention is not known but he obviously was 'cashing-in' on an invention produced long before the Civil War.

Scott in 1628 offered the invention of the leather gun to Gustavus Adolphus for £1,500 but it was not accepted. This might have been the type used in the English Civil War but there was another variety in use in Sweden. An Austrian, von Wurmbrandt, joined the Swedish army and actually made trials with leather guns in 1627. To give Scott his due, his guns were only half the weight of Wurmbrandt's and yet took a larger charge of gunpowder. As the King rewarded Wurmbrandt, he must have felt that the Austrian was responsible for the invention and had taken nothing from Scott.

Colonel Wemyss was Lieutenant-General of Ordnance and Train when Sir William Waller left London in December 1643 with wagons laden with leather guns. They were thought to be of very great use and were so light of carriage that one horse could draw a piece. The bullet cast weighed 1½ pounds and 'did execution very far'. Just before the Restoration Wemyss made a petition for the recognition of his invention.

Gustavus Adolphus is sometimes given the credit for these guns, but with little proof; yet there is little doubt that he used them extensively in the Thirty Years War where they produced the required effect of shock. Specimens still exist in Paris, England and Germany. These are easily distinguishable as Swedish by the fact that the lifting handles are made in the form of the letter 'G', for Gustavus. They were described in those days as 'composed of the most hardened leather, girt round with iron or brass hoops and could be brought to discharge ten times successively'. A gun in the Rotunda is attributed to Gustavus's troops. In this the centre is copper, tightly coiled round with hempen cord and bound outside with leather. The bronze trunnion ring placed at the centre has two light lifting handles. The one in Paris also has the copper tube, wired outside, and covered with leather.

The Scottish type was lighter in weight and 'of white iron, tinned and done about with leather and corded so they could serve for two or three discharges'. Such a weapon, which wore out so soon and possibly with unexpected results was not one to continue in popular use, although the city of Augsburg offered to the Emperor Joseph the First (1705–1711) one of these, now preserved in Vienna. It is said that they were discontinued after the battle of Leipzig, 1631, where they had become so hot that they discharged themselves spontaneously. The central tube screwed into a brass breech which was on occasion strengthened by strips of iron.

There was another country in which the leather gun was popular on account of its lightness. This was Switzerland, where it was welcomed because it could be man-carried in the mountains. This was as much as seven feet long—far larger than the usual Swedish pattern. Specimens are to be seen at Zürich, Hamburg and Berlin. The central tube of copper was encased in stone or lime before the leather was shrunk on.

As late as October 1788 a leather cannon was fired three times in King's Park Edinburgh, but it did not come back into the British Army.

The 'blinders' mentioned at the beginning of this section are referred to in other accounts as 'two barricadoes drawn on wheels, in each seven small brass and leathern guns charged with case shot.' Elsewhere the term 'waggonburgh' is used, and only one pair of wheels is mentioned. The inspiration seems to have come from the ancient ribaudequins or *tötenorgels*, the leather guns were the modern addition. How the Scots carried their leather cannon when they crossed the Tyne to invade England in 1640 is not known.

3. UNUSUAL MATERIALS AND TYPES

Accustomed as one is to hear of cannon barrels being made of metal it may come as a shock to know that wood has been employed for this purpose. Dire necessity brought this about during Auringzebe's campaigns in the Deccan. A besieged town had practically no artillery with which to defend itself, but the markets contained much wood and so the brilliant idea of making wooden cannon was conceived and carried out. The walls were lined with these imitation cannon and when the enemy did eventually appear and open fire, the wooden cannon also replied, shot for shot. It is true that only one discharge was necessary to destroy the mock cannon but the shot did go forth on its journey. Wood was also available in quantity and for each cannon expended a fresh one took its place. The besiegers did not discover the secret and eventually decided to abandon the siege.

The Paris Artillery Museum contains a wooden gun from Cochin China. The two halves are hollowed out of wood and banded together with iron strips. Whether this stood up to successive discharges is not clear. The Turks are also said to have had a cherry-wood cannon; and coming nearer to our own shores, we find that at the siege of Boulogne in 1544, Henry the Eighth used large wooden cannon. These were manœuvred across marshy ground and set up where the besiegers had deemed it impossible. The shock created when these large 'cannon' opened fire created panic. They are shown in the wall paintings at Cowdray House, and appear to be nearly two feet across the bore and about eight feet long. The secret of firing was the fact that another metal barrel was attached to the wooden one and this could fire. The idea seems to have been to overawe the enemy by deception. It is fascinating to note that according to a description written as early as 1588, in the Store Room of the Tower of London was a 'wooden gun mounted on a ship's carriage'. This gun was known as 'Policy' —whether an allusion to the false representation is not clear. Unfortunately the great fire of 1841 which lasted over four days destroyed this unique item.

A Swiss, Joseph Plattner, who visited the Tower in about 1599 writes 'next they did show us two great wooden pieces, the which King Henry VIII had placed on a marshy position over against the town of Boulogne, whereat the inhabitants were full of terror, for that they did think it to be a real battering ram, and could not imagine how it could have been got there on account of the soft ground and in consequence when they saw the strategy immediately surrendered the town.' It may be that the guides of the day supplied this coloured account in return for the four sets of gratuities which they extracted from visitors, but there is little doubt that these deceptive cannon were of use as they had been in the recent war.

During the Civil War of Cromwell's time, Lord Broghill took the Castle of Carrigadrohid in Cork by producing imitation cannon of wood. He used oxen to draw some large logs of wood in the fashion of cannon and so deceived the Irish that they parleyed and surrendered.

Imitation cannon known as Quaker guns were commonly used in the seventeenth and eighteenth centuries on merchant ships. No doubt they have been used on other occasions and will continue to be so, but one is unlikely to risk firing them, although examples of both flash and crash have been simulated in mock cannon.

From humble wood one can go to the most expensive materials. A Veronese arsenal had a great gun of gold and silver originally from Candia. Although silver models of guns are well known as trophies and mess ornaments, full-size versions made in silver are known in India. In Jaipur at the beginning of the century were bullock batteries with silver-plated guns. His Highness the Gaekwar of Baroda is credited not only with silver cannon but with a field battery of solid gold guns. Impressive though such a possession might be, it is hardly practical for war purposes.

Reverting to more practical warfare, there were very light cannon used at various times. Mobility was the desired end, but lightness of barrel brought about a very much smaller shot. The wooden carriage although somewhat lighter still remained cumbersome.

The *schlange* was a popular iron gun in Germanic countries about 1500. The falconets and robinets were small types of cannon in the orthodox manner, but occasionally unusual carriages were tried.

A short falconet in the Liechtenstein collection has a beautiful cast bronze barrel and is dated 1672. The carriage is light and spidery but ornate. The fore part is held up by wheels with a diameter of 26 inches, and the slim trail holds a built-in box. Another falconet at Woolwich has a very light barrel but large wheels. On the other hand, some Continental mountings had very slim front supports with very small wheels.

It would seem that the 'grasshopper' guns so widely used in America were made on these lines. On Staten Island in 1776 the Royal Artillery had four three-pounder guns mounted on grasshopper carriages and at Cowpens in 1781 were 'small field pieces called grasshoppers'. At the crossing of the Nive in 1813 two grasshoppers firing red-hot shot did good work for the Royal Artillery.

The galloper gun was the result of an idea to produce a gun light enough to be drawn at a gallop by possibly only one horse. The medieval inventors put their ideas on paper but the gun does not seem to have reached practical stages. Something may have been achieved in the Civil War but it was the eighteenth century which saw light field artillery in use. A French work of 1726 speaks of the Germans using these newly-devised guns which were made short and rifled. They fired an 8 or 4-pound shot. The trails were made in the form of shafts to take a horse. It is said that Frederick the Great used 3-pounders in his campaigns, mounted on galloper carriages. The British in Flanders in 1744 had them and used them with effect at Fontenoy. These six 1½-pounders of the Duke of Cumberland's artillery were drawn either by one horse or by two in tandem.

The *British Military Library*, a monthly publication, mentions that these guns were similar to those used to fire salutes in 1799 in St. James's Park on rejoicing days. They are still mentioned and depicted in a military dictionary of 1802. Abroad the galloper gun was used much later, with special success in the Bengal and Madras Armies. These were, however, not the trail and shaft combination but a light normal version of artillery as used in the horsed branch.

A galloping carriage was brought out again as late as 1898 when the Earl of Dundonald commanding the 2nd Life Guards invented a light steel and hickory carriage, for a Maxim gun which was to be drawn by one horse. The Life Guards took two

10—Galloper gun, eighteenth century.

of these carriages on official trials and although they endured rough handling, all tests were carried out successfully. Despite this success the idea was not generally adopted.

A peculiar gun was the Schuwalow, brought out by the Russians in the eighteenth century under Empress Elizabeth and named after the inventor Count Schuwalow. Small, chambered six-pounders were made with an eliptical bore. The object of this peculiar bore was to have the widest part placed horizontally so that the discharge of grapeshot or canister would spread in a horizontal direction against advancing humanity, and not be wasted either up in the air or down in the ground, Even in those days much fear was felt for the unknown powers of the Russians and thus when Frederick the Second of Prussia captured twenty-nine of this type in 1758 he attempted to dispel this fear by exhibiting them in public in Berlin to 'reveal the great Mystery of the Russians'. They were not considered of much practical value in Europe but a Dutchman made some for the Ruler of Kutch in India. These were cast in native iron and had a bore only 3¼ inches high but 28 inches wide. They were intended to fire canister, stones or iron bars but became no more than show pieces to be seen at Woolwich.

The siege of Gibraltar gave an opportunity for inventiveness on the part of the gunners. The Spanish floating batteries and fleet were constantly in the offing. The English guns fired from galleries in the Rock itself and it was found that the shots went over the enemy. To get sufficient depression, Lieutenant G. F. Koehler invented a special carriage. In some ways the invention recalled the early efforts of the fifteenth century. The barrel and bed were fixed together, hinged at the front end, and they rose at the back by means of two arcs. Needless to say the shot had to be well 'wadded' to stop it from rolling out. A similar idea had in fact appeared before. A German culverin of the fifteenth century was mounted on a four-wheeled platform and had two arcs for adjusting the elevation of the hinged piece.

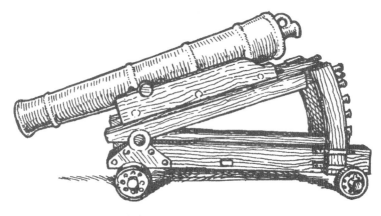

11—Gibraltar depressing carriage.

The opposite to a depressing carriage was the elevating carriage. More generally it was known as the disappearing carriage, but from its great cumbrousness the last thing it could do was disappear. Models of these are preserved at Woolwich. One from George the Second's reign has a pair of guns, each placed on jointed beams so that the barrel could be raised high up to fire over a parapet or wall; after which it could be lowered to the safer position on the four-wheeled carriage.

Another field of experimenting was (and still is) that of firing from sledge carriages. As early as the seventeenth century trials were being made to find carriages to take guns over snow and ice. Transportation caused little trouble but the snag arose when the moment came for the gun to be fired. The lack of friction with the ground surface did little to check recoil and the gun performed the most dangerous movements. But for all the difficulties, countries such as Canada have continually needed to emply some such method of conveying their artillery in winter.

4. DRAWN AND SELF-PROPELLED GUNS

Although horses are considered the normal method, many other ways of traction have been employed. Oxen and cattle, cheap and sturdy substitutes, were used extensively in the late middle ages. Oxen in the nineteenth century ousted the horse in India, though they were slow and not so easily manœuvred. It is in the East that unusual animals are employed as beasts of burden. Mules, notoriously bad-tempered, are sure footed in mountains and stony places. Thus they were admirable for batteries in which the gun was split into component parts with a piece on each animal. The idea of a segmented gun was also used in camel batteries. In January 1819 Captain I. H. Frith of the Madras Artillery raised a Camel Howitzer battery. These $4\frac{2}{5}$-inch howitzers which weighed 3 hundredweight were carried on a series of camels. The first had the barrel, the second the bed and another had the ammunition. It will be noted that these are more akin to mortars. The lascars who walked on foot assembled the howitzers at the appointed place. Then the European gunners who rode on horses dismounted to fire the guns—a very gentlemanly procedure. The battery was disbanded 15th May 1821.

Camels were also used for hauling small guns as early as 1835, and although a most awkward animal to train for such a purpose the Bikaner Battery was a success—a least for show purposes. So was the Jaipur Camel battery, at the end of the century, which pulled small muzzle-loading cannon.

By 1841 we have evidence that guns were hauled by elephants in India. The native states could not resist using them for the same purpose, and richly caparisoned the huge beasts. The British forces used elephants in the successful engagement of Ali Musjid in 1879. Elephants were capable of pulling the most heavy loads but under gun-fire were most unreliable. It is little wonder that at the end of the nineteenth century, experiments were being made with steam traction, which was unlovely but reliable in action. Although used for very heavy guns, steam engines did not entirely replace horses and it was not until after the First World War that the petrol engine brought about its drastic change.

Apart from using animals for haulage or draught, at various times the inventors thought of using animals to carry the actual weapon and to be a kind of carriage. Needless to say it was from the East that the first idea came, on—of all animals—the ungainly camel. It had been pressed into service early in the nineteenth century and even at the end of the century Jaipur had its camel batteries with long swivel guns mounted in front of the humps while the gunners sat behind.

Colonel Charles Gold who served in the East may have been inspired by this idea, for in 1814 he produced a 'proposal for a new kind of Horse Artillery: the gun to be mounted and fired from the Animal'. This manuscript of 1814 shows a horse very much encumbered with harness. The saddle is set well back towards the hind-quarters and the pommel is extended to a stout framework. On this is a fixture to permit the gun to swivel and go up and down. The gun barrel was to be 3 feet long with a 2-inch bore, to weigh about 50 pounds and fire a ball or a pound of grapeshot. Many straps went around the horse's chest with the intention of taking up the recoil. This was the great problem and one has visions, after a salvo, of a row of animals on their backs with their feet in the air. The only animal capable of being a suitable carriage for a firearm seems to be the human one.

One problem of mobility in gunnery was that of firing when in motion. There were many essays and ideas throughout the ages but no permanency came until the invention of the petrol-engine which opened the way for armoured cars, tanks and 'self-propelled' artillery.

Movement in the late middle ages was attained by use of men or horses. Thus one fifteenth-century idea shows a large two-wheeled cannon being pushed by a horse. The trail is made like shafts and the gunner sits on a platform in front of the horse's head ready to fire the gun. There is a large spear in front, a heavy wooden shield over all, to say nothing of a driver on the horse. The humans might survive a discharge but the shock to the horse can only be imagined. The man-handled ribaudequins and *orgelgeschutze* could be fired when advancing although no account can be given of such an action.

A gun cart of about 1520 is depicted in an engraving by Ludwig von Eyb. It may not have been his own invention, but this four-wheeled wagon like a mobile fort has a large gun in front. The gunners operate in the dark interior while the motive power is supplied at the rear by armed horses straining on a shaft and swingle-trees placed in what might be called the opposite direction to normal. An actual example of one of these moving forts seems to have been in use by the Duke of Albany in 1523. Spies' accounts tell of carts covered with steel and brass each with eight guns and men, and each cart moved by armoured horses so that the cart 'goeth backwards'.

Leonardo da Vinci and other men of inventive minds produced their own versions of movable forts which are not quite in our line. One idea which can hardly be omitted is that of Agostino Ramelli who in 1588 published an engraving of a battle wagon which not only was propelled by a man turning a handle but could also take to water and be moved by a paddle wheel. But we do not hear that tides of battle were turned by this amazing invention so possibly it progressed no farther than paper.

On 3rd March 1693 James Austen and Francis Bull took out a patent for a machine or chariot of artillery 'which is Musket Proofe and soe contrived as to hold falknetts or small field pieces and two hand mortars to be used by the party sitting in the chariot'. But no practical details are forthcoming.

Gabriel Bodenehr in 1760 conceived a gun-carriage to be propelled by foot power and using a large gun. Mid-eighteenth century, a French Engineer officer, M. de Bonneville worked out the idea of a light wagon carrying a gun weighing over 1½ hundredweight firing a 1-pound lead ball. The *canonier* was to sit at the breech end and load and fire 'while the horses went at a gallop'.

A well-known man was Mr. Sadler of Pimlico 'a very ingenious machinist who not only had his own body of Sharpshooters but was the inventor of a celebrated War Chariot'. In 1798 Thomas Rowlandson the famous caricaturist produced a coloured print showing the elegant four-wheeled chariot 'in which two persons advancing or retreating can manage two

12—Sadler's Flying Artillery.

pieces of ordnance (3-pounders) with alacrity and in safety so as to do execution at the distance of two furlongs'. Actually there was a third person who drove the two horses—at full gallop according to the engraving. The two gunners perched high in the air each have a gun. Mounted on a circular platform they can be turned in any direction. To load, the short barrel is tilted vertically with the muzzle uppermost. As a consideration to the driver, a device stops the cannon from being depressed too far and a plate over his head is obviously designed to protect him from muzzle-blast.

The famous hunter, Colonel Peter Hawker, also had his ideas on this subject as appears from a small model at the Rotunda, Woolwich. It is a breech-loading swivel-gun mounted on a four-wheeled carriage to be drawn by either horse or man.

But full realization of the ambition to load and fire when moving on land was delayed until the twentieth century, though armoured trains and machine guns on wheels were some way towards it. The full use of 'self-propelled' guns only came in the recent war.

IV

MACHINE-GUNS

~~~~~~

I. FIRST ATTEMPTS AT MULTIPLE FIRE

THE word 'machine-gun' is a modern one but the principle that it involves was practised in most ancient times. The idea that a number of projectiles would leave the launcher with the speed of a machine was applied in the days of arrows when the 'polybolos' was invented. Whereas the present system involves one barrel with a quantity of amunition, the inventors of the middle ages had to rely on a multiplicity of barrels.

It would appear that the multiple gun was among the earliest inventions, even challenging the cannon. The pot-of-fire or the vase, made entirely of metal, has good evidence of its antiquity whereas the cannon made up of long bars and rings comes in a little later. The first weapons must logically be small. The bronze casting as found in Sweden could not be safely held in the hand. The simplest way of fixing must have been to secure it to a firm bed, and so small an object on a large wooden block would only invite the addition of similar items. We know that there existed such a weapon—the ribaudequin, the ancestor of the machine-gun.

The name ribaudequin had been in use before the invention of gunpowder, just as many of the early names applied to fire-arms had been used for other purposes. The ribaudequin, a descendant of the scythed chariot, was a two-wheeled cart which had a large bow to fire javelins, quarrels or pellets. Some writers claim that tubes of Greek fire were also used on the

74

ribaudequin. Designed for the defence of narrow passages or paths to which it could be quickly wheeled, extra protection was given by the addition of spikes, pikes and other sharp weapons. The invention of firearms only brought another type of weapon to be added to the accommodating carriage.

An account of 1339 mentions these ribaudequins and a payment to a metal worker of St. Omer in 1342 for a stay to strengthen the timber under the engine; and from the same source we learn that it was to carry ten cannon. It is curious that accounts from Bruges in Belgium also mention payment for iron straps to clamp the 'ribauds' to the carts which are referred to as 'niewen enginen'.

The English were not slow on this occasion to take up the new invention. Peter van Vullaere, a *maitre des ribaudequins* at Bruges in 1339, took service with the English force that invaded France in 1345-6, but before the Great Expedition set sail much activity and preparation took place in England. In February 1345 King Edward the Third ordered guns and pellets to be assembled. No less than one hundred ribauds were to be made 'pro passagio Regis versus Normanniam', and for the next six months wood wheels and axles were collected by Robert de Mildenhall, the Keeper of the Tower Wardrobe. These ribaudequins were made at the Tower of London by the King's own workmen.

The bills for the ingredients of the gunpowder are in accounts rendered after the Great Expedition had sailed, and even more tantalizing is the fact that we have no proof of these weapons in service until the siege of Calais in 1347. Although no doubt useful as siege pieces, one cannot prevent a wishful thought which takes them to such battles as Crécy. While most siege equipment faced the town and was intended for its reduction, the purpose of these inventions was to face the opposite way and to fire on an enemy attacking from the rear. That they performed this duty successfully is to be noted in the fact that when Philip of Valois, leader of the French Army, had knowledge of their presence in an army which he intended to attack, he declined to engage in close combat and withdrew.

The *Annual Year Book for the Administration of Ghent* showed in 1347 that these ribaudequins were already in common use, no doubt in defensive rôles such as the siege of Tournai where they were employed to command a gateway.

Froissart gives a description of the ribaudequins belonging to the Gantois in 1382, and by them they were used against the Comte de Flandres. There were 5,000 men who charged with 200 of these carts, to defeat the army of 40,000 men who attacked Bruges. They were high-wheeled barrows having long iron pikes, projecting in front when they accompanied the troops in battle-array. Napoleon the Third in his studies on artillery says that the ribaudequins were the first artillery of fire in battles and that the tubes threw small leaden balls or quarrels.

If the weight of shot from the small tubes was very little, the users of this invention hoped to achieve results by the multiplication of the barrels. One Italian account tells of 144 of these small bombards being mounted on one block so arranged as to fire thirty-six at one time and arranged in three tiers. It needed one separate gunner for each tier and four strong horses to pull the cart. An interesting contrast to modern times when one man is expected to do similar duty. Three of these monstrous affairs were made in 1387 for Antonia della Scale, the Lord of Verona.

Juvenal des Ursins in his *History of Charles VI, King of France* tells us that in 1411 the Duke of Burgundy had with his army of 40,000 men not only 4,000 cannon but also 2,000 ribaudequins—a high proportion if he writes truly. Monstrelet writing of the same army, says that there were a great number of ribaudequins drawn by horses. They had two wheels, a mantle or shield of wood and one or two veuglaires, as well as the usual spiked defences. For the moment the idea of multi-guns was in abeyance. The veuglaires or breech-loading cannon were very necessary, for if muzzle-loaded cannon were used the gunner would have to expose himself by going to the front of the cart.

The shield of wood was necessary to protect the gunners while loading their guns and also to protect them when actually advancing their machine in the face of the enemy. Some later illustrations show horses reversed in their shafts pushing the carts forward, a practice which appears to be liable to high casualties. A Latin manuscript in the Paris Bibliothèque Nationale, 'Pauli Saventini Ducensis tractus de re militari et de machinis bellicus', shows one which although captured by the Turks was returned from Constantinople to Louvoin in 1688. It was a two-wheeled affair, had scythes and the shaft between the two horses was prolonged to carry a 'port-fire'.

In the early fifteenth century the term ribaudequin was no longer being applied to the cart with the cannon, but to fire-arms such as the *arquebus-en-croc* which was used for defending passages and also on carts occasionally. But the old idea of the ribaudequin reappears as the organ, orgue or *Orgelgeschütze*, whose name makes us imagine the close rows of gun-barrels like organ-pipes playing a tune of death. In fact they were also known as *Todtenorgel*—organs of death.

The Museum of Sigmaringen has an *Orgelgeschütze* of the mid-fifteenth century with five muzzle-loading barrels. These serpentine cannon are of wrought iron and appear a clumsy development of the original idea. Nicholas Glochenthon who made illustrations of the Armouries of Maximilian the Great in about 1505 shows a serpentine organ of forty cannon, all packed together in a solid mass. He also shows one of the old type of vehicle with spears and sharp projections all round a fine metal shield which goes over the top to protect four bronze guns with curved stocks.

It may be mentioned at this point that there also existed a contraption known as a 'waggonburgh' which although strictly not a multiple firing weapon was a variation of the ribaudequin. The waggonburgh was a kind of mobile shed on a four-wheeled cart in which were a number of separate and independently mounted cannon. In action, flaps in the sides were lifted up to permit the cannon to fire. Usually the waggonburghs were drawn up in a loose circle around the encamped army and acted as a temporary fortress wall.

Needless to say, Henry the Eighth had his own distinctive ideas about gun carts. They are to be seen in old prints, after the wall paintings of the siege of Boulogne. These two-wheeled barrows had shafts for pushing forward by hand. There is over all a long shield shaped like half a cone, the forepart ending in spikes. The two cannon which partly projected through this shield were operated from the shelter of the cover. A list of the Army in 1544 included '55 gunners appointed to the shrympes with two cases each'. The humour of the time identified these peculiar inventions with lowly shell-fish and is reminiscent of the later parallel when armoured fighting vehicles were called 'tanks'.

The use of the organ in the battlefield had been mainly in the defence of the bodies of bowmen, but when they dropped out of fashion so did the organ and its associates. In the Tower inventories for 1575 were 200 engines capable of discharging twenty-four bullets at one time, but the German Zeughaus had a late sixteenth-century affair with sixty-four barrels which must have had a terrific expenditure of bullets.

It appears that the Low Countries kept the word 'ribaudequin' in use quite late, possibly because they originated it. The men of Maestricht when besieged in 1579 by the troops of the Prince of Parma victoriously defended the breaches in their ramparts made by Spanish cannon-balls, by means of these ribaudequins. They are described as two-wheeled carriages holding rows of arquebus-cannon.

The Swiss constructed about 1614 some organ-pieces called *greleuses*—hail-makers, on account of the vast numbers of projectiles which they fired. These were fired by means of a single channel of priming powder. The tendency to place these instruments on wheeled carriages and to arm them with long iron pikes led them to be nicknamed 'hedgehogs'.

Even the term 'organ' was becoming obsolete and in England a 'barricade' came to mean a similar device. Incidentally, by 1630 'ribaudequin' had come to mean a standard size of gun-barrel. The English Civil War saw a type of multiple gun in action, and Clarendon in his *History of the Great Rebellion* informs us that the Cavaliers at Copredy Bridge in 1644 captured two barricadoes of wood which were drawn upon wheels and on each were 'seven small brass and leather cannon'.[1] In a contemporary account these barricadoes were also known as 'waggonburghs', no doubt a recollection of the more ancient title.

There is a model of a *Totenorgel* from about 1670 in the Liechtenstein Collection in Vaduz, which has a triangular block with three groups of twelve tubes. Each time a group was fired by a central touchhole, it could be turned to the next

[1]See page 63.

face with its group of barrels. Military writers of the late seventeenth century were still fascinated by 'organs', and Montecuculli in his *Memoirs* wrote that 'organs are many cannons assembled together on a carriage of two wheels, which go off with a single touch of fire. They are charged at the breech with their chambers'. This shows that breech-loaders were still in use. An inventory of Hesdin in Artois dated 1689 included an organ of twelve musket cannon, but before the end of the century the term organ was no longer being applied to battery fire but to battering rams. The weapons used for defending narrow passages or doorways were now single light cannon or heavy wall-pieces on a light mobile mounting with wheels on the front supports.[1]

Multiple barrels combined in one gun had been tried, as in the three-barrelled weapon of Henry the Eighth's time and also the triple-barrelled French cannon of Marlborough's time, but they belong rather to the story of cannon. The other line of approach was to make a number of charges come from a single barrel. We can understand the revolver principle used in early try-outs but the inventions of the Marquis of Worcester are not so clear. In 1663 this gentleman claimed that he had a way of placing six muskets upon a carriage shooting 'with such expedition, as without danger one may charge, level and discharge them sixty times in a minute, two or three together'. Two years later he offered 'a cannon of four pieces which can discharge 200 bullets in an hour and a cannon that will discharge bullets twenty times in six minutes' but leaving the barrel so cool that 'a pound of butter would not melt on the breech'. We are left wondering what these weird inventions may have entailed, but another invention of the same period is not so difficult. This is the 'fiery dragon' patented by Drummond of Hawthornden, which consisted of many barrels fastened together on one machine. The Tower Inventory for 1687 included 'an Engine of 160 musquet barrels' which may have been something on the foregoing lines. Also listed were engines of six and twelve barrels supposed to have been taken from the rebellious forces of the Duke of Monmouth at Sedgemoor in 1685.

[1]See page 151.

2. PUCKLE'S REVOLVING GUN

One pioneer in the field of invention who produced a machine-gun that progressed beyond the stage of theory was an Englishman named James Puckle, born in Charles the Second's reign and dying in 1724. A prolific writer, he was by profession a solicitor or, in the phrase of those days, a Notary Public. Not only do the illustrations and details of his gun appear in the specification No. 418 of 1718 in the Patent Office, but his first trial iron piece and his completed gun were preserved by the Duke of Buccleuch and sent to the Tower of London. The gun, called in the specification a 'Defence', was fitted on a 'trepied' or tripod of surprisingly modern appearance. The top part turned laterally and freely in a tube attachment. Sighting or vertical movement was achieved by a 'curb and crane', but the most important part of the invention was the separate cylinders which took anything from six to nine chambers. A crank movement brought the chambers one by one to the breech and a half turn was used to make a tight grip. Each chamber had a flink-lock attachment for firing and the projectiles were various. There were 'round shot for Christians', square bullets for use against 'Turks' and even a 'grenado' made up with twenty square bullets. Apart from these Christian sentiments, the cylinders were marked with a patriotic couplet, engravings of King George, Britannia and the Holy Bible.

At this period there were many get-rich-quick schemes and Puckle was doing nothing strange in launching a company for his invention, the shares in which in 1720 were valued at £8 each. A public trial was made of the machine-gun, and the *London Journal* of 31st March 1722 recorded that 'Mr. Puckle's Machine' was discharged sixty-three times in seven minutes by one man, in the rain. But even this fine performance did not lead to immediate success, for the machine-gun was not put into production and a broadsheet commented that 'they're only wounded who have shares therein'.

But other inventors were not dismayed. The pursuit of an endless stream of bullets continued. A revolver-gun in the Tower, engraved on the plate 'Durlachs 1739', had four barrels to be revolved by hand, but this was still the old scheme of multiple barrels. A Swiss inventor, Welton, in 1742 made a

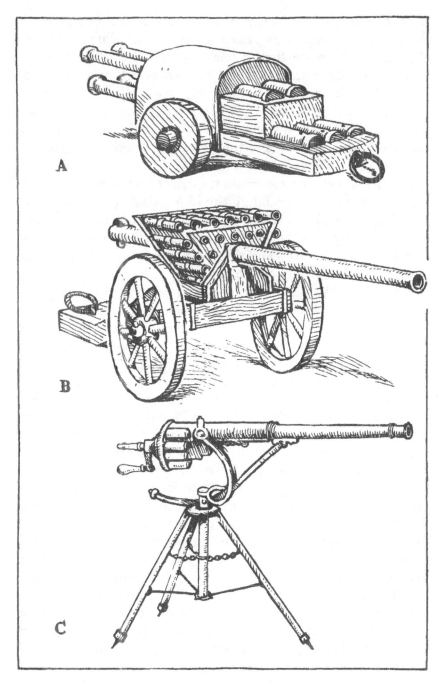

13—A. Organ gun, fifteenth century. B. Serpentine organ, seventeenth century. C. Puckle's machine-gun.

small cannon of copper which had a slot at the touch-end of the barrel. Through this passed a large panel which held ten charges, each to be fired when opposite the bore. Even a Dutch inventor in the middle of the eighteenth century could think of nothing better than going back to the old tried favourites and constructed an engine which had twenty-four barrels in four rows of six, each of which could be set off by a flint-lock. This late version of an organ is preserved in the Arsenal at Delft.

Further attempts were made to perfect revolvers, and when Nelson was killed a special gun to clear fighting-tops was produced by a British gunsmith, Nock. This had one central barrel surrounded by six others. The flint-lock igniter sent the spark first to the centre barrel and then to the six outer ones. This was a kind of mass fire and only a curiosity.

A thirty-one barrelled machine had been brought to England from Paris in 1815 and a smooth-bore gun taking eighteen chambers had been invented by General Josiah Gorgas, an American. It is of interest to note that when Samuel Colt, an American, brought a lawsuit against the Massachusetts Arms Company for infringing his patents, they suggested that Colt was not the inventor of the revolver system but Puckle. They produced a model made up after the Patent Office specification but it was insufficient to prove their case. One wonders what would have happened had the finished brass pattern come to light in time to be produced in court.

The supremacy of continental invention was being challenged by the rapidly-growing American nation. Practical work was being accomplished rather than the odd curiosity. In 1861 the Billinghurst Requa Battery gun was being made at Rochester, New York, and was used practically in the American Civil War where it had its début in the attack on Fort Sumter, Charleston, South Carolina in 1864. The battery had twenty-five barrels which fired simultaneously and were elevated by means of a central screw with a cross-turning head. Mounted as it was, on two light wheels, it bore a similarity to the 'organs' of the fourteenth and fifteenth century. For all that it was not much of an advance in the field of rapid fire.

In 1862 another American, Dr. Richard J. Gatling of North Carolina, patented a very successful battery or machine-gun.

The principle was to have four to ten rifled barrels rotating around a central axis by means of a crank. A multiplicity of barrels was employed to avoid overheating. The bullets were continuous and gravity fed from a trough and fired as long as the handle turned or until the apparatus jammed. This weapon was used in the defence of the James River in the American Civil War where it replaced the Requa. It was adopted by the British Government in 1871 and used in the Zulu war. But its liability to jam did not make it a popular weapon.

The Gatling gun continued in use in different theatres of war and various models with varying calibres were introduced. By 1876 a five-barrelled .45 model was firing at the rate of 700 rounds a minute and even up to 1,000 in a short burst.

Less than twenty years later, the Gatling was electrically driven and firing at the rate of 3,000 rounds per minute. The system of multiple barrels was successful from the point of view of rapid fire and coolness but the weight of the many barrels was a great drawback, and thus when a single barrel could be made to take large quantities of ammunition the Gatling gun disappeared. But the Gatling had a long war service—the Ashanti campaign of 1874, the Zulu war, and in the Sudan with Kitchener. Its use against white folk was not thought quite right but the Gatling gun during its time served in America, China, Japan, Turkey, and Russia. In fact in Russia it was so popular that it was manufactured there and called the Goroloff gun after the officer who supervised the copying.

The Nordenfeldt was another multiple-barrel gun, moving laterally. It was an engineer, H. Palmcrantz, who invented the system in 1873, but it was financed by Thorston Nordenfeldt a Swedish banker in London. The number of barrels varied from three to six. In the three-barrelled version twenty-seven cartridges were on a wooden strip which could feed the gun at a rate of 350 shots per minute. The Gatling had jammed because of the type of cartridges used, but Boxer brass cartridges were used with the Nordenfeldt and the trouble did not arise. The Gatling did not go out of fashion at once, but the Navy in 1881 took up the Nordenfeldt gun extensively on torpedo boats and found it of great value in the operations in Egypt in 1884.

The gun invented by Captain William Gardner of the U.S. Army was produced in about 1876 on the Nordenfeldt principle and although at first furnished with several barrels eventually became a single-barrel variety, with a better loading device. The first patterns had trays with thirty-one cartridges mounted on wood. A useful point about this machine-gun was its mounting, admirably suited for firing over a parapet. The cartridges were fed from a vertical clip and could fire either singly or at a speed of 120 rounds per minute, depending on the speed at which the crank was turned. The Gardner was used widely in the British Army prior to the adoption of the Maxim gun. It was one of the 'portable' machine-guns. With its tripod and 1,000 rounds of ammunition it weighed less than 200 pounds and could be carried on a horse.

A very famous example of multi-barrelled guns was the French mitrailleuse. A Belgian engineer, Joseph Montigny of Fontaine l'Eveque near Brussels, made the gun after an original idea by Captain Faschamps, also a Belgian. Napoleon the Third was most impressed by this weapon which looked like a field gun but contained thirty-seven (later twenty-five) rifle barrels, loaded simultaneously with a plate of thirty-seven (or twenty-five) cartridges. The turning of a crank released one firing pin after another and up to twelve plates of clips could be fired a minute, making up to 444 rounds per minute. The British never adopted this gun, because in tests the Gatling gun made a much better performance. But the French put their trust in these mitrailleuses, originally called *canon à bras*. In the Franco-Prussian war of 1870 where they were used like cannon, the Prussian knocked them out at the first opportunity and they were never used to the full extent of their powers. The French had thought that they had a 'secret' weapon but the Prussians had all the information they required and the Bavarian troops even had guns of similar pattern. The original Montigny guns were used from 1851 to 1869 when the French Government manufactured them after adopting various improvements made by Colonel De Reffye. It was a useful enough gun when employed against massed infantry but not the substitute for heavy artillery which the French tried to make it.

3. THE MAXIM GUN

Hiram S. Maxim, originally an American born in Maine but later a naturalized British subject, did much work in Europe and produced a gun on a new principle—a true pioneer striking out on an entirely fresh path which led, for once, to full success and knighthood. In his younger days he had been made fully aware of the effects of the recoil from a military rifle. The tremendous waste of energy had impressed itself on his mind, and he was able to put the thought to a useful application. He had been exhibiting electrical inventions at an Electrical Exhibition in Paris when a fellow countryman suggested that much money could be made by finding means for Europeans to get more easily and quickly at one another's throats. Maxim was already a rich man with a capable engineering staff and he decided to use the idea of employing the energy of a gun's recoil to reload itself. Thus in 1881 he came to London and evolved a gun which he claimed as totally new because no one had previously thought of one gun which would load and fire itself. Existing apparatus was of no use to him and so in early 1884 he constructed the mechanism which appeared in the South Kensington Museum labelled 'This apparatus loads and fires itself by the force of its own recoil and is the first apparatus ever made in the world in which energy from the burning powder is employed for loading and firing the arm'. His method of loading was by a belt, an innovation, and he also employed the daring idea of mounting the gun on a tripod instead of wheels. His gun was considered a great wonder.

But visitors came from far and wide, even Lord Wolseley the Duke of Cambridge and high-ranking War Office staff, in order to see the gun fire. At the trials the very large quantity of 200,000 rounds was fired. The unusually rapid rate of fire was not necessarily a selling point. Indeed the King of Denmark and an envoy from China were dismayed at the expenditure of cartridges which cost at the rate of £5 per minute and decided that such a gun was far too expensive for their countries. But this gun was not a "flash in the pan'. The British Government wished to be the first to give him an order and specified that the gun must not weigh more than 100 pounds, and that it should fire 400 rounds per minute. To this, the inventor responded by producing a 40-pound gun firing 2,000 rounds in 3 minutes. The original version underwent modifications and improvements but the original system remained. As long as the gunner held his finger on the trigger the recoil extracted the fired case, let a fresh round slip into place, and then fired that; and so on until all the rounds were expended or the trigger released. The excessive rate of fire heated the barrel but a water-cooled jacket solved this complication. After 600 rounds were fired, the water would begin to boil and evaporate, so that a supply of $1\frac{1}{2}$ pints was needed for every 1,000 rounds.

These maxim guns, produced by the Vickers-Maxim Factory, were used extensively in the First World War during which time Maxim died—in 1915. A lighter version had been made weighing only 25 pounds, or 50 pounds complete with the tripod. It could be carried on horseback and differed from the heavier type by being air-cooled instead of water-cooled. The Vickers M.G. Mark I was produced in November 1912 and weighed $28\frac{1}{2}$ pounds without water. This is the type still in use after two world wars. It is about half the weight of the original gun, has a pressed steel water-jacket instead of one of bronze, and utilizes a gas-trap recoil-cup at the muzzle to speed up the fire of the .303 cartridges. The Germans and the Russians both later used the Maxim on their own peculiar mountings.

The idea of using the wasted energy released by the gases of an exploded cartridge was employed in another fashion by a different invention. A Viennese, Captain Baron A. Odkolek von Augezd, designed a weapon which allowed the gas to escape from a vent in the barrel to operate a piston and cylinder. By this method the cartridge was extracted and a fresh one inserted.

An American, Benjamin Berkley Hotchkiss, originally from Connecticut, made weapons at St. Denis near Paris in 1875 including a gun much like a Gatling; but he improved on the idea mainly by using explosive and large shells. In trials against the Nordenfeldt gun in 1876 the palms went to the latter. But the Hotchkiss gun was improved by using a single barrel and have an escape-port to make the gases drive the breech action, the loading and ejection. It was then capable of firing over 600 rounds a minute and over-heating occurred in the barrel.

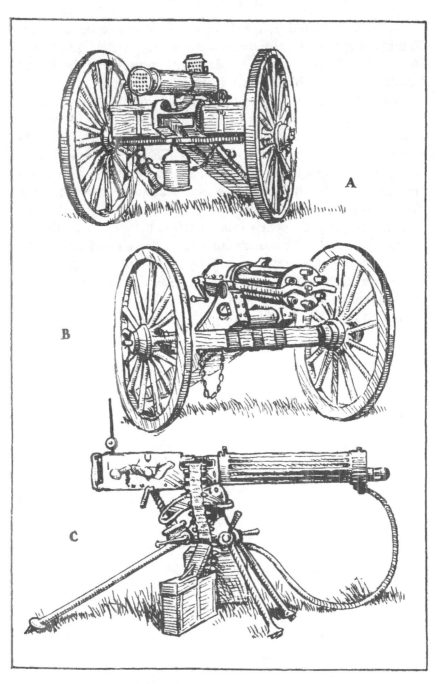

14—A. De Reffye Mitrailleuse. B. Gatling gun. C. Maxim gun.

Cooling was effected by air deflected by wings or flanges. The French adopted the Hotchkiss and used it in the First World War as did the Americans, the Indians, and some of the British cavalry. The Hotchkiss is still in use.

James Moses Browning was another who saw the value of escape gases. He was born in 1875 as the son of an American gunsmith and was brought up to the trade. In 1889 when he noted the effect of muzzle-blast on foliage, he conceived a method of using the escape gases. By mounting a cone at the muzzle of a rifle, he made the blast carry the cone forward. As this cone was connected to a light rod, the breech-block was moved also. Six years later in 1895 his idea was adopted by the Colt Arms Company for use in the United States. An improved design produced a fully-automatic gun fed by a 250-round canvas belt. A hole in the bottom of the barrel struck a piston down and to the rear, which unlocked the breech and extracted the shell. It is famous for its use in aircraft.

V

HANDGUNS, MUSKETS AND RIFLES

〜〜〜〜〜〜〜〜〜〜〜〜〜〜〜〜〜〜〜〜〜〜

I. THE SMOOTH BORE

THE idea of a portable firearm seems to have occurred very early to the pioneers of this new field of invention. The ancestor of the rifle can be traced back to the earliest trends of development. The small tubes on the ribaude-quins were potential handguns. It would have been a very easy step to mount one of these small cannon on a staff of wood. The difficulty is to find the exact time of the introduction. In Italy there were two handguns which in the last century were claimed as the oldest then known. One was of cast bronze with a date 1322 and the initials 'PPPF': it was also ornamented with oak leaves and a Greek cross, all of which make it seem to be in a very advanced state of development and probably not among the first ever made. The other specimen was of wrought iron, and little is known about it. There is said to be in Namur an example with bars of iron forged in the same manner as the larger cannon; but the earlier handguns are not usually forged but cast. Another feature of the handguns was that they did not have the separate breech chamber, but were closed at the end.

For written evidence, the town of Perugia in 1364 ordered 500 little bombards which were to be portable and fired from the hand. Each was to be no longer than the palm of one hand or approximately nine inches. Although some experts claim that these are early pistols, the firer could hardly have held the unprotected iron in his bare hand at a time when it was dangerous to fire even a hafted weapon. It is most likely that these small bombards were put on wooden supports or shafts. The town of Modena in the same year also acquired 'four little scioppi for the hand', and these Italian guns are said to have been cast in bronze. 'For the hand' means that they are held by hand and not resting on the ground like the larger cannon.

According to Froissart, the English troops led by Sir John Chandos carried such hand cannon before Montsac in 1369 1369 and there is an early mention of these weapons (about 1374) in a bill of William de Sleaford, Keeper of the Privy Wardrobe in which 13 shillings are paid for fitting eight guns with helves after the fashion of pikes. It has been stated that these were the 'gonnes' used by the forty armed men who attacked the Manor House at Hunterscombe, near the Abbey of Dorchester, Yorkshire, in 1375, but sufficient evidence is lacking.

There is preserved in the Swedish State Historical Museum a small bronze gun found at Löshult near the North Sea. This is a cast object with a touch-hole leading through to the central cavity. There is also a reinforcing ring at the muzzle. As there are no projections it must have been held to its bed or staff by means of a metal band, for this also could not be held in the hand. It appears to fit the description of the Perugia bombards mentioned above.

In 1381 thirty hand cannon are recorded at Augsburg, and Froissart quotes the French soldiers as using 'bombardes portatives' against the people of Liege a year later. The term 'handgun' appears in 1386 when Ralph Hutton sent three to the Chamberlain of Berwick. Possibly the same articles are meant in one of his accounts which mentions 'baculos curtos et grosses ligatos cum ferro pro iv cannonibus parvis'. Forty-eight *hand-büchsen* (handguns) are mentioned as being in Nuremberg in 1388.

An early German MS. of about 1390 describes how to load guns. Three-fifths of the barrel is to be filled with gunpowder. It is to be rammed down, but a space should be left before inserting the wooden plug, after which the ball is inserted. The term 'hand coulverin' in use at the time also indicates a close connexion with the heavier artillery. These hand coulverins were too heavy to be handled by one man and needed two, one for the holding and aiming while the second did the firing.

An improvement in fixing a small gun to its staff was to hollow half its shape in the wood and have it partly embedded before strapping it down. One such example preserved in a German museum is on these lines and has a long wooden stock making the over-all length nearly five feet.

Specimens preserved in Berne and Prague before the war had yet another improvement—the gun was made with a hollow section at the touch-end so that the wooden stock could actually fit into the metalwork. The first shapes of barrels were simple tubes but before the end of the fourteenth century the finish and style of the metalwork had improved and became in some cases works of art. In the ruins of a castle near Tannenburg in Hesse was found a well-made cast brass gun which must date from before 1399 because the castle, a robbers' stronghold, was thoroughly destroyed in that year. The elegant barrel is thicker at the gunpowder chamber and has a reinforcing band at the muzzle. The weight is $2\frac{3}{4}$ pounds, with a bore of $\frac{7}{16}$ inch; and although this part measured $12\frac{1}{2}$ inches it was made to fit on to a long haft.

Another bronze casting on somewhat similar lines but much smaller—only 8 inches—is to be seen in Sweden. In the main it is octagonal and fits on a shaft but it is highly ornamented, having lettering on the sides and a most unusual feature on the top, a fully modelled head with beard. Below is a hooklike projection which would serve to take up the recoil if the firearm were placed against a wall.

There are contemporary illustrations showing early hand cannon in use, and because they are obviously difficult to handle away from a wall they are shown with the long shaft planted in the ground, while the fore part is held up either by hand or by means of a prop. Thus the recoil would go into the ground and even by this method it is thought that two men would be necessary to fire the piece.

Another way of attaching the gun to its stock was to have a tang or prong upon the metal work and insert that into the woodwork. There is preserved in Namur Museum a cast iron gun of this principle.

An inventory of 1397 listing the military stores in the City of Bologna includes 'item—viii sclopos de ferro de quibus sunt tres a manibus'. Literally the word 'sclopus' means a noise and

was applied generally to firearms, but the additional information 'three for the hand' can only mean three handguns.
'Sclopus' was not forgotten in the nineteenth century when the
word 'scloppetaria' was used to indicate the science of firearms
—the art of 'noise-making'.

There is an illustration in a Gottingen manuscript of 1405
showing a man firing one of these early handguns. The whole
weapon must have been 8 feet long. One end is on the ground
and the other is held up by a long fork three or four feet long,
thrust into the ground. The soldier, well covered against possible
disaster, leans forward to ignite the gunpowder by means of a
bent and red-hot wire.

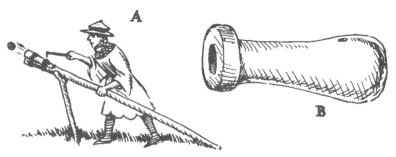

15—A. Handgun, fifteenth century. B. Swedish handgun, fourteenth century.

This high angle of fire or trajectory, although suitable for a
battle-field or in the open, was of little use in defensive or high
places, and thus the addition of a hook below permitted a secure
fixing against a wall or through a window. These were known
as wall-pieces and remained in use for many years. Frequently
they were of a heavy calibre but they always retained their
archaic appearance. The length was sometimes tremendous,
like the one of 10 feet in the Liechtenstein Collection at Vaduz.

The handgun planted in the ground or used as a wall piece
was still not suitable for active movement on a battle-field and
so the next step was to make the haft quite short. The improvement of quality and the proportions of powder permitted less
cumbersome weapons. The wooden part was now held between
the elbow and the body. As skill increased, the position was
changed to the shoulder. An etching by Israel von Mechlin in
about 1420 shows this firearm being used in a curious manner.
It is being fired by a devil at the Saviour in a Resurrection

scene! No doubt the artist was sure that gunpowder was the invention of the devil. With the shift of position to the shoulder, the shaft-like end was found unsatisfactory and it was broadened into a butt end to rest against the firer; but the troops in the Siege of Arras in 1414 are said to have still used the shaft between arm and body.

The straight axis of the butt or stock against the body made too violent a shock, and the next advance, made by an unknown inventor, was to make the stock curved. Thus the recoil was indirect and caused it to waste its excess energy by throwing the gun upwards. One French expert gives the credit to the Swiss in 1392 for this innovation, but a much later date seems more probable.

It may be appropriate to mention here that although handguns tended to be muzzle-loaded there were attempts at breechloading. There is a specimen, said to have been in the Tower of London but not traceable there now. This was cast entirely of iron; at one end was the barrel, at the other a stout handle. In the centre was a depression which took a rectangular box to contain the charge but the method of fixing is not clear, and in the absence of the example it is difficult to assess its value.

The touch-hole of hand guns was originally on the top, as with large cannon, but it was eventually placed on the right side, where also an area was devoted to the 'pan' or ledge where the priming powder was placed. Ignition, by means of a hot coal in tongs or by a red-hot wire, had its drawbacks and the introduction of burning match produced a more satisfactory method. Match was cord or twisted material soaked in saltpetre or lees of wine which burnt slowly and steadily. Direct application to the touch-hole by hand must have presented a source of danger to the soldier and an indirect method was sought and found. A pair of jaws held the burning match and a long piece of metal was attached to the handgun by means of a pivot in the middle. Raising the end at the butt brought the fore end with the match down into the pan. At last it was possible for one man to manage a piece on his own with a certain amount of safety. The holder was much used in about 1424 and was called variously a 'dog', 'serpentine' or 'dragon' from its shape or fancied appearance.

The Duke of Orleans in 1411 had 4,000 men armed with

handguns; but England seems to have been more modest, for the purchases for the Holy Land in 1446 included two handguns at 4 shillings. The Paston letters of 1459 also mention handguns, but the first organized band of handgun men to operate in England is generally claimed to be the 300 Flemish mercenaries who were hired to fight with Edward the Fourth and came over to England in the Wars of the Roses. Their services in the campaigns of 1471 suffered because of the stormy weather which put out their matches and dampened their gunpowder. It is said that Charles of Burgundy lent these men to Edward because the two men were brothers-in-law. The Swiss also saw the value of the new weapon, for at the battle of Morat in 1476 there were 6,000 culverins, obviously not the full size cannon but possibly a large version of handgun.

Henry of Richmond is said to have had foreign hirelings armed with handguns in his battle for a crown in 1485. Although the English preferred the bowmen for battle, there is in a Harlian manuscript some mention of 'hacquebuts' in an order to the Constable of the Tower.

The handgun was changing shape, from a crude object to a piece of machinery—the matchlock or arquebus. This weapon is said to have appeared in the second quarter of the fifteenth century. The distinguishing feature is usually accepted as being the trigger to depress and raise the match; but illustrations by an Italian, Martin, *circa* 1469 show the *archibuso* as a straight-hafted gun of three to four feet in length, whereas the *schioppi* is a shorter weapon distinguished by a match in a serpentine. It is difficult to decide whence the name came, for variants were in use at the same time throughout Europe. There was hackbuss, hakbüsch, arquebus, archibuso, and arcabouza. Several nations claim to have been the originator. For example, the Italian arca-bugio or -bucca means a hollow bow. The cross-bow which was sometimes called an arquebus had a similar butt and trigger arrangement to release the projectile. Some cross-bows even fired leaden bullets. Thus the replacement of a metal barrel instead of the bow on a cross-bow made the firearm. The German term *hak-büchse* can be translated as hook-gun, and could refer to the curved jaws of the matchholder. It is a fact that a *doppelhaken* is a double match-lock. These *doppelhaken* had two serpentines or cocks with separate

94

triggers aimed at the same touch-hole, the idea being that if one of them misfired then the second might bring success.

Two fine examples of early harquebuses or arquebuses are preserved in the Tower of London. They had dragon-shaped serpentines and a down-curving butt. The pans have pivoted covers. One has a V-shaped backsight but the other has the innovation of a tubular peepsight at the back—an idea only 'rediscovered' in modern times.

The many spellings of similar terms make confusion in sharply defining these early types, and although verbally the hacquebut has a similar appearance, it is held to be a different kind of firearm; in fact its stock was altered to a hooked or crooked butt. This later developed into a very curved butt which when put on the shoulder, placed the barrel high and was supposed to bring the gun to eye-level for aiming.

The hacquebut was known in the reign of Richard the Third and called variously, even in England, hackbuss, hagbutt and hakbutt. It was slightly smaller than the normal handgun which was 3 feet long, but the hagbut by decree of the third year or Henry the Eighth was not to be under ¾ yard, inclusive. The demi-haques and half-haquebuts of the same period were more akin to long pistols.

The arquebus-à-croc definitely has a French origin because of the last part of the name, which indicates a hook or projection below the barrel for large guns, mentioned above, to take up the recoil against a wall.

Although it has been stated that when Henry the Seventh created his Yeomen of the Guard he equipped half of them with bows and arrows and half with harquebuses, there is no evidence of their firearms until 1544 when it was stated that the King was accompanied by twenty-five archers on the right side and as many gunners on the left side. Henry the Eighth, we are not surprised to learn, did much for the progress of firearms. In 1511 he paid Lewis and Alexander de la Fava £200 for 500 hakebusses. The next year Peter Grey was ordered to provide 420 handguns with bottles and moulds for the Army then preparing for war.

The Guild of Saint George, still in being as the Honourable Artillery Company, was established in 1537 and encouraged by Henry the Eighth as a Fraternity of Artillery of Long Bows,

16—Sixteenth-century handgun.

Cross Bows and Hand Guns, which acknowledged that the long popular archery had a new rival. A proclamation of 12th January of the same year ordered that all handguns carried by licensed persons were to be 2½ feet long on the stick. A later law of 1541 encouraged gentlemen and above to keep handguns 'of length of one whole yard and not under' so that they might become adept at shooting. In striking contrast to Queen Elizabeth who later did all she could to encourage her subjects in the cheaper art of archery, Henry did all he could to encourage firearms and he published in February of 1544 another Proclamation inviting his subjects to be skilled and trained in using handguns and hagbusses, and permitted all over the age of 16 years of age to use these arms without fine. However, others than gentlemen got hold of these new weapons and a further Edict had to be published stating that 'Murders, robberies, riots and routs with crossbows, little short hand-guns and little haquebuts have become rife—' and, elsewhere little handguns were spoken of as being 'readily furnished with quarrels, gunpowder, fire and touch'.

As late as 1560 the term handgun was still being used, for Sir Thomas Gresham imported 1,500 handguns costing 7 shillings each from Antwerp. Sir Roger Williams at about the same date notes that 'for the recoyling there is no hurt if they be straight stocked after the Spanish fashion—were they stocked crooked after the French manner to be discharged on the breast, few or none could abide their recoyling, but being discharged from the shoulder after the Spanish manner there is neither danger nor hurte'.

When the externally pivoted match-holder gave place to the trigger-type, the spring and other mechanism was placed inside the woodwork and protected from the elements. The mechanism was known as a lock, each type having its own name. One pattern in use up to 1520 was the button lock. Pressure on a button placed under the stock let the cock and match fall into the pan. A type manufactured in about 1521 by Cornelius Johann can be seen in the Tower of London. This has a spring and catch. When the cock is pulled back, it is held under pressure until the catch releases it on its duty. A later type of the Elizabethan period, instead of having the burning match held in the jaws of the cock had a piece of tinder. But this had to be ignited by match before firing.

A new term, 'Musket', had appeared by 1530 in Italy. The origin of the word is obscure. As many larger firearms were named after creatures, so the use of the word 'moschetto' or 'musket' meaning the male young of the sparrowhawk appears a most probable answer. However, Italy makes an early claim to an inventor of the name of Moschetta of Feltro. A Spanish origin is also suggested in the use of the word *moscas* or *mosquas* meaning sparks from a light, while yet another claim cites Russia, or Muscovy as it was then called, as the country of origin.

There are muskets at Dresden dated 1570 and 1573, and the first to appear in France were so heavy that they had to be fired from a rest. The musket originally was not popular in England but by 1570 military writers who had seen its uses in the fighting on the Continent were advocating its use. Thus a list of equipment issued in 1577 to troops sent to aid the Dutch included 'muskets with flasks and rests'.

For once the Germans had to be content to use a military word of foreign origin and a Wurzburg inventory of 1584 contains *muscaten, halbe-musketen* and *doppel-musketen*. In 1588 the citizens of Norwich paid 27s. each for English muskets including the rest, flask and 'touch-box'. By 1620 the price was reduced to £1. os. 8d. and in 1632 the musket was priced at 15s. 6d., 10d. the rest and 2s. 6d. for the bandolier.

At the beginning of the seventeenth century the musket was still a large weapon, for Sir Thomas Kellie in 1623 tells us that its barrel was 4 feet long and carried a bore of twelve bullets to the pound.

But the musket was improved and made lighter so that by the time of the English Civil War the rest was no longer necessary. The old name continued in use, to refer to the commoner types of shoulder firearms, until the rifled musket became so popular that it could be referred to just as a 'rifle'. It was then that the old term dropped out of use and the non-rifled weapons became known as smooth-bores and shot-guns because the small shot used in hunting could not be used advantageously in rifled barrels.

Always while one line of invention was being exploited, another line was being developed. The inconvenience of keeping a piece of hempen rope alight and ready for long periods of time, led to the use of a new material, pyrites. This mineral substance, a natural combination of sulphur and iron, had been well known for centuries past for its quality in making sparks, and so a mechanism was devised to employ it in firearms.

The earliest existing gun using this material is, or was, in the Museum at Dresden. This example was once called the original invention of Father Schwartz and is still referred to as the *Münchsbüchse*—or the Monk's gun. There is little doubt that it was made much later, probably in the early part of the sixteenth century. It consists of a tube about eleven inches long and 3¾ inches in diameter. A ring of iron pulls the rasp or file-like surface over the pyrites. The sparks thus created ignite the gunpowder.

The next stage of development was to replace the rasp by a more controllable device, and the wheel-lock came into being. In this type of lock the yellow pyrites was held in a pair of jaws against a toothed wheel. The pull of a trigger released a spring, which in turn pulled a fine chain wound round the axis of the wheel. The resultant stream of sparks was directed at the exposed priming powder. The wheel-lock was then rewound by means of a key or spanner carried separately.

Obviously the wheel-lock was a delicate piece of work and could only be afforded by rich men, so it was not generally used. A defect on the battle-field was the fact that the pyrites might break into pieces at the most inconvenient moment. The process was perhaps invented in Nuremberg in 1517, but precise evidence is, as usual, lacking. There is no doubt that Leonardo not only wrote a description of a wheel-lock but that he claims to have shot doves with it. All early specimens of the wheel-lock are German, and many were made in Nuremberg with dates from about 1541 on the locks.

Its introduction into England was slow. The rich noblemen

of the Elizabethan era could afford to have their specimens made with elaborate stocks and fanciful engraving but the common soldiery had to be content with matchlocks. Haquebuts were fitted with the wheel-lock mechanism but they were not for the common rank and file.

It is true that the cavalry found a need for the wheel-lock to be applied to their pistols and carbines because of the difficulty of handling the matchlock mounted. It was the German Reiters who took this mechanism up for their pistols and revolutionized cavalry tactics but in England the sword remained the standard cavalry weapon. But leaders who had fought in the continental wars or those who could afford them were proud to possess wheel-lock weapons, and although much respected as hunting weapons, they eventually gave place in England to the more sturdy and cheaper flintlock or snaphaunce. The Continent continued to favour the more complex weapon but by the end of the seventeenth century the wheel-lock was out of use.

Another type of firearm was the caliver which came into prominence during the Elizabethan era. It was a lighter kind of matchlock, between a harquebus and a musket in weight, and fired without a rest. It is an English Militia officer, Edmund York who gives us the origin of the term. He tells us that in Piedmont where he served in his younger days each regiment of infantry had a different calibre of harquebus, but that before the battle of Moncontour in 1569 'the Prynces of Religion caused 7,000 harquebuses to be made all of one calibre, which was called the "harquebuze de calibre de Monsieur le Prince".'

The great advantage of this weapon was the fact that the size of shot was standardized and could be used in any of these calivers. Its popularity at the time can be gauged from the fact that in 1578 the Tower of London had 7,000 in store. It was not an expensive weapon and the cost per caliver which in 1574 was 14s. dropped to 13s. 4d. in 1581.

Although the first calivers appear to have been weapons other than the normal harquebus, the term eventually was used to mean a light weapon which could be fired without a rest. It was almost despised and thought to be the only fit weapon for such unfit soldiers as Wart, according to Falstaff's statement in *King Henry IV*, Part II.

These calivers did not have the exaggerated curved butt of the hackbutt, and were nearly straight with a 42-inch barrel. Sir Roger Williams in his *Brief Discourse of Warre*, 1590, speaks of calivers being able to fire twice as quickly as muskets but, of course, doing less than half the damage. He suggested that there was no harm from the recoil if they had straight stocks and were fired from the shoulder. But if they had crooked stocks like the French and also fired from the chest then 'none could abide by their recoyling'.

Despite the great advance in the lighter firearms on the Continent, Queen Elizabeth issued many orders for the encouragement of archery in preference to gunnery. It may have been for the reason of economy, but the bow was fighting a losing battle and at last in 1595 the Trained Bands of London were ordered to exchange their bows for calivers and muskets.

The caliver and bandolier were valued at 14s. 10d. in 1620 but the caliver suffered an eclipse in the Thirty Years War when the musket was taken into popular use on account of its heavier shot which could pierce armour. The use of a musket-rest was necessary, but that was no deterrent and gradually the caliver disappeared from the field of battle.

The weakness of pyrites led gunsmiths and inventors to seek a stronger material. Flint supplied the answer and could even be used in the wheel-lock mechanism. Existing examples present a difficulty in defining a clear difference between the original wheel-lock and the flintlock or conversions, but it was soon found that the flint could not only take a stronger lock but needed one. The wound-up wheel was not necessary and in fact suffered harm when used with the stout flint. Thus a new idea came into use. The jaws or cock, which held the pyrites originally and now the flint, were still employed but operated by means of a spring. In place of the wheel with its toothed edge was a piece of steel with serrated ridges on its face. The new lock was known as the *Schnapphahn* or snaphaunce. The derivation of the word is from the likeness of the flint-holder to a 'pecking cock'. It has been said that the snaphaunce was named after chicken thieves, robbers and marauders who were truly known by that name; but the rogues who preferred the safety of the flintlock to the betraying light on the match were named after the weapon and not vice versa. Snaphaunce weapons were said to have been allocated to troops proceeding to Ireland in 1580.

Some weapons in an early inventory of the Tower of London are referred to as 'firelocks', but from their elaborate description and high value this would appear to mean wheel-locks. This fact is mentioned to show the difficulty of identifying contemporary weapons by a name which is sometimes given a different meaning in modern times.

The flintlock is held by some to be a different invention from the snaphaunce and dated about 1630, but others hold that it is no more than a slight rearrangement of the parts already in use, with the addition of the 'frizzen' or battery. It is a point of manufacturing rather than invention but the old-established matchlock still continued as the standard weapon for the common soldier during the English Civil War, and even as late as the Monmouth Rebellion in 1685 it was still in use. One reads that the betraying lights of the burning matches at night could also be used to advantage and for camouflage, when pieces of burning matches left in rows on a hedge conveyed the impression that musketeers still lined the defences even though they had silently crept away.

Snaphaunces had been manufactured in England as early as 1608 when guns and carbines were sent to Phillip of Spain as a gift from James the First. It will be noticed that the bore or diameter of the barrel is frequently calculated on the number of bullets to the pound, and in the long directions accompanying the rates to be charged by the English gunsmiths in 1631 is the information that a barrel 4 feet long should take 'the bullet of ten in the pound standing and twelve rowleing', meaning that the larger one would fit tightly but the smaller would just roll out.

The matchlock was also added to flintlock muskets as an alternative if one system failed to work. The flintlock now had the pan-cover as part of the striking surface and was of a pattern so well designed that it continued in use until the nineteenth century. It was also possible to convert matchlock muskets into flintlock ones and there are warrants still in being from the Duke of Albemarle, from February and April, 1660, for the matchlock muskets of his regiment to be converted to fusils (or flintlocks). The bore was also altered to take bullets of fourteen to the pound.

Flintlocks had been issued to selected groups such as the storming parties in the Civil War, or for the special bodies of Fusiliers necessary to guard artillery or ammunition where the sparks from a lighted match might cause disaster. Grenadiers, when they were introduced late in Charles the Second's reign, were issued with fusils. There are flintlocks in the Tower of London and in private possession which have the lock engraved with 'I2R' with a crown over them to indicate James the Second's cipher. One of these was made by Brooke, a well-known gunsmith, and his flintlock musket has a barrel of 31 inches. This is the lighter fusil or carbine barrel but the matchlock had a barrel of 42 inches. This was in accordance with the order of 1680 but four years later 3 feet 8 inches is quoted for the sanguined (or reddened) barrels of snaphaunces.

Slings were now added to flintlock muskets and to the variety known as fusils, whose barrels were now stated to be 3 feet 2 inches long. The name 'fusil' had already been in use many years on the Continent and took its origin from 'focile' meaning fire. It had been found that dragoons (who were now no more than mounted infantrymen) and grenadiers (who needed both hands free to operate and throw their grenades) were encumbered by the ordinary flintlock, but the addition of a broad sling permitted them to sling the firearm over the back and leave the hands free. Eventually the sling was added to all muskets, when the problem of expense was overcome in William the Third's reign. Then the flintlock became the common weapon and the matchlock disappeared.

The term 'Brown Bess' came into use about this time and meant a musket. Certain people have tried to connect the phrase with Queen Elizabeth, but she had died many years before the expression was used. Actually the reason was much more mundane, for the 'brown' merely described the colour and 'Bess', rather than coming romantically from a woman's name, is connected with the German or Dutch word for gun—*Büchse* or *buss*, no doubt brought to England by the Dutch troops who came over with William and who were still in the country.

The flintlock musket had reached a standard of perfection,

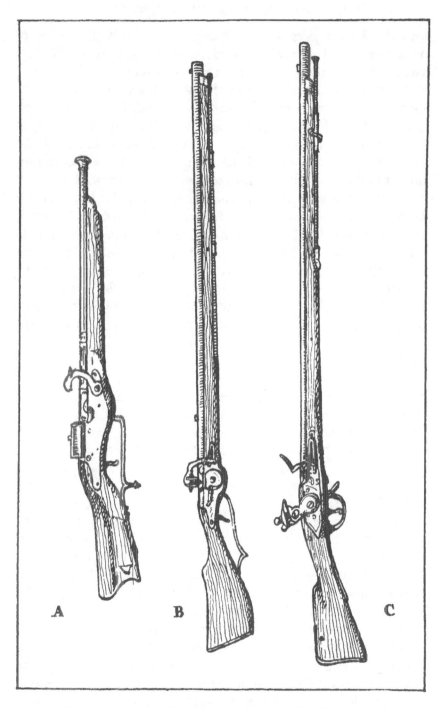

17—A. Breechloading matchlock musket. B. Wheel-lock musket. C. Flint-lock musket.

and the Brown Bess was the weapon that won the Battle of Waterloo and was not replaced until the advent of the percussion lock in 1830, a century and a half later.

There were other experiments and developments but we must trace the smooth-bore musket to its end. It received a new lease of life when the percussion lock was developed. This great step was mainly brought about by the research of the Reverend Forsyth and is dealt with more fully in the section on ammunition. The fulminates had been known for their extreme explosive powers but they could not replace gunpowder because their action was too violent. Forsyth must be given the credit for seeing in the fulminates a new method of detonating. He produced his prototype in the summer of 1805 by converting a flintlock. The next year he worked on a military model in the Tower precincts, but upon being dismissed by the hasty Earl of Chatham went into business for himself, an odd occupation for a parson. His idea was basically good and was constantly being pirated and exploited, but it was never taken up by the Government in its original form.

It was the adoption of the copper cap to hold the detonating material which first made the idea of value to the Army. Various gunsmiths have claimed the credit for the cap but Joshua Shaw seems to have the best claim. In 1814 he had a steel cap in which, the fulminate pellet was renewed as each shot was fired. Next he made his caps of pewter and this time they were deemed expendible, and in 1816 he adopted a cap made of sheet copper.

Many more years were to elapse before the British Government decided to look into the possibilities of the percussion-lock. It was not until 1834 that trials were carried out at Woolwich and it was found that the new weapon had a much better performance than the flintlock musket. It was the Brunswick rifle which in 1836 was accepted by an Ordnance Board at Woolwich, but the rifle was another development and to follow that we must retrace our steps. The smooth-bore musket did not go out of use at once, for with true economy the old flintlocks were converted to percussion locks and remained in use until 1859 at least as a military weapon. But this was a policy of economy for the most part, and the smooth-bore was latterly produced as a shot-gun and used for hunting.

2. RIFLED FIREARMS

There were inventors who brought in a new idea and others who discovered an old idea, and endeavoured to bring it up-to-date. From the earliest times rifling had been tried, then forgotten, then brought back again, left out of favour and finally vindicated.

The rifling of hand firearms is said to have been invented towards the end of the fifteenth century, in Leipzig in 1498 according to some and in Vienna by Gaspar Kollner or Zollner according to others. Little sure evidence is forthcoming for either statement. Augustus Kotter or Kutter of Nuremberg is said to have used rifling in 1520 but as there are rifles dated 1616 with the same name, in a Paris museum, one wonders whether there may not be some confusion of thought. A seven-grooved gun by Kutter is at Woolwich.

These straight rifled grooves were intended to counter the heavy fouling of the barrel due to the crude gunpowder of those days, which burnt so imperfectly. But early in the sixteenth century pitched rifling (intended to rotate the projectile) was introduced. The theory of centrifugal force, used to keep the projectile on a steady course, was understood but the expense of rifling was too great to permit it to become a general process.

A Zurich inventory of 1544 lists a rifled gun and at Woolwich is a gun with a grooved barrel said to have come from Hungary. The Viennese collection of weapons has several dated between 1550 and 1560.

Sir Hugh Plat, the writer of the *Jewel House of Art and Nature* in 1594, gives details of how to make 'eight gutters somewhat deep in the inside of the barrel and the bullet a thought bigger than the bore'. This latter was to be rammed in and driven down with a 'skowering stick'.

It is said that the Danish troops of Christian the Fourth were the first to be armed with this weapon and a gun-barrel of this nation dated 1611 is preserved at Woolwich. An English patent 'to rifle, cut out and screw barrels' was granted to A. Rotispen on 24th June, 1635, which indicates a late arrival of the new invention in the country. A Madrid book of 1644 showed that experiments were being made in the twist of rifling by trying a half turn, a full turn and even one and a half turns in the length of a barrel. Seven to nine grooves were employed. No doubt it was the problem of expense which prevented rifled weapons being taken up extensively by the regular forces. The French were proud to remark that their Royal Horse Guards had eight rifled carbines per troop.

18—Typical 4-groove rifling.

In the middle of the eighteenth century Benjamin Robbins, a member of the Royal Society in London, read a learned paper on the theory of rifling but little practical result came of his correct deductions. The English weapon had settled down to an established pattern and changed little. In the wars in America the backwoodsman knew full well the value of his sporting rifle and used it effectively on many occasions to defeat the disciplined British infantry. But the lesson was not learnt by the authorities at home, and even the American Government was still establishing factories to make smooth-bore arms in the last years of the century.

The American rifle was a small-bore development from the hunting rifle taken to that continent by the Germans. The German huntsman used a heavy musket with a large bullet but the Americans claimed an advance in the methods of loading, which was to use a patch. The Germans when they dropped their bullet in the muzzle made it grip the grooves by using a heavy rammer to flatten it out (and also spoil its ballistic qualities). The American principle was to use a small patch of leather well greased, which partly enveloped the lead ball. This could be rammed down the barrel in an easy action without damage to the shape of the ball. The German method not only distorted the projectile but even permitted an escape of gas. The American idea of greasing made for better firing, for the expanding gases forced the patch and grease to make a tight fit, and the ball was projected forward without distortion.

The American rifle is frequently called the Kentucky, but this is not truly named for the weapon was originally produced in Lancaster, Pennsylvania, and in the few surrounding towns. The ball used was originally sixteen to twenty to the pound but later decreased to thirty-six to the pound, according to Colonel Hanger, a noted rifleman of the period. This gentleman who was a close friend of Tarleton and writer of *To All Sportsmen* was later the Fourth Baron Coleraine but during the American War was the Captain of a Hessian Jäger Corps and knew the advantages of a rifled barrel. But the continental rifle was of heavy make and although fitted with a hair trigger and occasionally telescopic sights, was clumsy to handle. The British Government did not mind employing mercenaries with rifles but did not produce the new guns officially. In fact it was left for a volunteer officer, Ferguson, to create the first British rifle unit.

Although there are pioneers who blaze a trail for others to follow, often there are those who show the way without recognition and have their work neglected. Such a man was Patrick Ferguson. For years soldiers had been handicapped by the complicated loading of their muskets, mainly by reason of many ingredients which had to be inserted at the narrow muzzle-end of the barrel. The advent of the successful breech-loader would solve that difficulty and it was Captain Ferguson who invented such a weapon. It was produced in quantity, used to very good purpose in actual warfare, and its inventor died because his enemies found it too effective. And despite this good record, the authorities permitted the rifle to drop out of use.

The striking feature of this rifle was the perpendicular breech-plug, which being threaded, dropped down when the trigger-guard was turned round. The ball and charge were placed in the exposed breech. Then a turn on the guard in the reverse direction twisted the plug upwards, thus sealing the barrel and making it ready for firing.

The *Annual Register* of 1st June, 1776 had a long account of the experiments with a 'rifle gun' upon a new construction by Captain Ferguson, which were made at Woolwich before Lord Townsend, the Master General of the Ordnance, Lord Amherst, General Harvey and other high-ranking officers. The trials were severe. To quote this periodical, this gentleman 'under the disadvantages of a heavy rain and a high wind performed the following four things, none of which had ever before been accomplished with any other small arms:

1st, He fired during four or five minutes at a target, at 200 yards distance, at the rate of four shots each minute. 2nd, He fired six shots in one minute. 3rd He fired four times per minute, advancing at the same time at the rate of four miles in the hour. 4thly, He poured a bottle of water into the pan and barrel of the piece when loaded, so as to wet every grain of the powder, and in less than half a minute fired with her as well as ever, without extracting the ball. He also hit the bull's eye at 100 yards lying with his back on the ground; and notwithstanding the unequalness of the wind and wetness of the weather, he only missed the target three times during the whole course of the experiments.'

It was not until Ferguson volunteered for service in America that he had the opportunity to command a corps of Volunteers equipped with his invention, the first organized troops of any country to have a breech-loading rifle. His small body of a hundred men so effectively 'scoured the ground that there was not a shot to annoy the column on its march' to the Battle of Brandywine in September 1777. Unfortunately, in later fighting a bullet from an American rifleman shattered his elbow; and while Ferguson was thus incapacitated, Sir William Howe the Commander in Chief disbanded the Corps and had the rifles put in store.

But Patrick Ferguson soon commanded another corps, this time as the lieutenant-colonel of the American Volunteers. These Sharpshooters from New York and New Jersey were also armed with the Ferguson rifle. During an advance to South Carolina with a column, about 800 strong and mainly loyalist Militia, he was surrounded at King's Mountain by American forces said to number 3,000. Bitter fighting gradually reduced the small force. Ferguson fell with eight bullets in his body. His corps was wiped out and his rifles disappeared, no doubt valuable prizes for the victors, who knew only too well their effectiveness.

American authors have written that 'had Great Britain manufactured more of the Ferguson rifles, perhaps he would have gained further victories' but the authorities did nothing further regarding that excellent breech-loading firearm and over ninety years elapsed before the breech-loader came again into service, the new pattern being the converted Enfield-Snider issued to infantry in 1871.

Of the original weapons, fewer remain in existence than can be numbered on one's fingers, but they still serve to show the lost opportunity of the powers-that-were at that period. An inquisitive American has tested one of these rarities. He found that the speed of loading and other qualities were confirmed. During the practice firing, three shots in succession at 90 feet at a $1\frac{5}{8}$-inch bull's-eye, came respectively within $\frac{1}{2}$ inch, 4 inches and $1\frac{3}{4}$ inches: a very good record indeed.

Rifles were accepted into the British Army, almost by accident. Four hundred of Hompesch's Mounted Riflemen were drafted into the newly raised 5th Battalion of the 60th Regiment of Foot in December 1797. They brought with them their distinctive uniforms of green and their German rifles. The 60th Foot had made an attempt, nearly forty years before, to obtain rifles; but it was the popularity of the rifle with the foreign corps serving in British pay that broke down resistance to the new weapon. There were units with such strange names as Hardy's Rifle Regiment, Löwenstein's Jägers and so on, but the first complete regiment to be equipped as riflemen was the Rifle Brigade which began life as the Experimental Corps of Riflemen. It was in January 1800 that the Duke of York called for men from fourteen regiments of the line to form the new body which was equipped with the Baker rifle.

Ezekiel Baker was an English gunsmith who had produced rifles for sportsmen and had published a book called *Remarks on Rifled Guns*. Trials of his weapon were satisfactory and despite the extra expense it was taken up by the Army. The Baker rifle had seven grooves in which the bullet took a quarter turn as it went along the 30-inch barrel. Being a muzzle-loader the soft lead ball, when dropped down the barrel on top of the gunpowder, had to be tapped by a ramrod and mallet. Thus the lead was forced sideways to grip the grooves. After a short time the mallet was discontinued and the heavy ramrod was found sufficient to achieve the necessary result. The butt of this rifled musket had a brass plate which covered a hollow space used to contain the greased patches to be rammed home with every bullet.

The first pattern Baker rifle had been made with a .65 calibre which was smaller than the standard one then in use. In 1807 a second Baker was produced, this time to take the service ammunition of .74 calibre. Later, about 1830, the bore was changed back to the original dimension. Although the Baker rifle was considered a suitable weapon to be issued to all riflemen and specialists, the main body of the infantry had to be content with smooth-bore muskets, most probably because of the expense involved in a complete change-over, although many commanding officers felt that there was no need for accurate shooting. Volley or shock effects were deemed necessary and time spent in loading rifles would be wasted.

But as usual, progress had been made outside the military sphere. Fulminating powders had been 'tamed' and used for setting off the gunpowder. This is discussed more fully in the section on Ammunition. Most gunsmiths had hoped to discover in the fulminates a powerful substitute for gunpowder, but when gun after gun blew up they abandoned the search. The Reverend Forsyth was not dismayed with burst barrels, but proceeded to find a new method—that of detonating the gunpowder. His flask which released a few grains at a time *did* work but was a trifle cumbersome. Other pioneers tried the new idea in different guises, such as pellets, paper caps (like those still in use today for toy guns), tubes and other methods. But when the copper cap came along, then the British Government was ready to take up the idea. It was Captain Berners of a Jäger Regiment in the Brunswick Army who proposed a rifle with two deep rounded grooves which made one turn in the length of the barrel. The Brunswick rifle had a larger bore than the Baker and had a special bullet with a belt around its middle to fit the grooves. A board at Woolwich examined several weapons in 1836 and adopted the Brunswick in place of the Baker. The new gun was the first percussion rifle to be generally adopted in the British army although a few Baker rifles were converted. This firearm remained in use up to the Crimean War but it fouled badly and in its time was called the worst military rifle in Europe.

The percussion system having been established, inventors

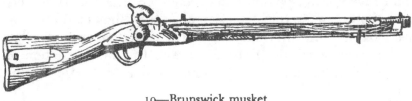

19—Brunswick musket.

took to investigating another aspect—the shape of the bore. A famous huntsman, Colonel Beaufoy, had in 1808 advocated the use of an oval bore with an increasing twist—the idea being to impart a greater twist and subsequently a more accurately aimed ball.

A square bore had been tried in Germany, a seven-sided one in Nuremberg, and in addition a hexagonal bore had been tried centuries before. This latter was once again proposed in 1839 by J. M. Moore, R.A. It was eventually adopted by Sir Joseph Whitworth for his rifle of the 1857 trials but had no universal appeal. An octagonal bore was tried by that famous engineer Sir Isambard Brunel and this too had no permanent effect.

More popular was the oval bore. Captain Berners, already mentioned, is said to have applied the idea to the Brunswick rifle but the inventor who used the oval barrel with the best success was Charles Lancaster. Working in New Bond Street, London, he used the idea extensively and later his rifle was taken up by the British Army.

Then we come upon an improved projectile. Captain Minie of the Chasseurs d'Orleans—the Rifle Brigade of France—was an instructor at the School of Musketry at Vincennes. He had experimented in 1847 with a bullet containing an iron cup in its hollowed base. On being fired the gases forced the cup into the bullet, making the sides spread out to form a gas-tight fit. The French Government quickly adopted this idea (the rifles were issued to Minie's own regiment) and the British Government were pleased to produce the rifle musket pattern in 1851. Captain Minie was paid £20,000 for his patent. A further claim was made by Greener, a well-known Birmingham gunmaker who produced evidence that he had offered a patent bullet on the same principle as early as 1836 to the British Government. The Government had accepted trials at the cost of the inventor in 1836 but had rejected the principle. However, after the liberal payment to Captain Minie they could hardly overlook the inventor on their own doorstep and in 1857 Greener was granted £1,000 for 'the first public suggestion of the principle of expansion, commonly called the Minie principle'.

The new .702 Minie rifle had four grooves with a less violent twist than that of the Brunswick. Some of the smooth bore 1842 muskets were converted and rifled with three grooves. This 'sea-service' pattern was issued to the Royal Marines. For the first time it was intended to issue rifles to all infantrymen and most of those who left for the Crimean War in 1854 had them, but complete re-equipment never took place owing to the advent of the Enfield rifle.

Viscount Hardinge, Master General of the Ordnance, ordered a series of experiments to take place at Enfield in 1852 at which leading manufacturers were encouraged to send examples of their best work. The result, the Enfield rifle, was adopted in 1853 and contained the best features from each. The import of complicated American machinery expanded the Royal Small Arms Factory at Enfield to make the new weapon. The new weapon actually contained little new in the way of principles but had all the refinements and finish which kept it the standard infantry firearm from 1855 until a breech-loading rifle was adopted in about 1866–7. It was this weapon which replaced the Minie Percussion Rifle in the Crimean War, and it was later issued to Indian troops. It was the cartridge of this new rifle which was greased with cow's fat and so acted as an additional cause of the Indian Mutiny.

Trials at Hythe in October 1853 between the Enfield three-grooved rifle, the Minie pattern of 1831 and the Lancaster elliptical-bore rifle with an increasing spiral resulted in favour of the latter. This must have caused consternation and further trials took place during the next month. This time the Lancaster was found to be 'wanting'. The projectile was discovered to have a tendency to 'strip' in the barrel. Thus in 1855 although not condemned out-of-hand this elliptical-bore rifle with a barrel of 2 feet 8 inches was relegated to the Corps of Sappers and Miners, who later became the Royal Engineers, and does not figure again in our story.

The Commander-in-Chief of the Army in 1854 had asked Sir Joseph Whitworth to study the subject of rifled barrels. After many trials a hexagonal barrel was developed with which either hexagonal or cylindrical bullets could be used—Shades of Puckle arise! The successful trials of 1857, in which this gun was tested at Enfield against the Enfield rifle, produced a report in 1862 complimenting Mr. Whitworth, as he was then, on the superiority and accuracy of his rifle. Production proceeded at a leisurely pace and in 1864 the Whitworth rifle was issued to the 4th Battalion of the Rifle Brigade but never became a general issue. The Whitworth rifle was thought sufficiently worthy to be the one selected for Her Majesty Queen Victoria to fire when she opened the First Meeting of the National Rifle Association at Wimbledon on 1st July, 1860. It was fixed to a rest and when Her Majesty pulled a lanyard it hit a target at 400 yards, within one and a half inches of the centre.

Many smooth-bore muskets had been converted to rifles, but the improvement of the cartridge with a self-contained system of ignition opened the way for the breech-loader, although the smooth-bore muzzle-loading musket remained in use up to 1859 and the muzzle-loading rifle up to 1867.

3. BREECH-LOADING GUNS

It is said by some authorities that the Army was content to carry on with out-of-date muzzle-loaders. Something new might lead to changes in the arms-drill, considered a precious part of the infantryman's life. But the great Volunteer Movement of 1859–60 brought thousands of civilians in contact with the service weapon and it was found wanting. Private weapons were pressed into service and the impetus towards improvement soon led to the adoption of the breech-loader.

The 'revolutionary' introduction of a breech-loading mechanism had its origins in the earliest days of firearms, and although never completely forgotten it had lain in limbo and was now coming back as a permanent feature. The defect had been the lack of precision fitting of the breech, allowing an escape of gases which would be dangerous to the firer. It is interesting to trace the path of the breech-loader which goes back to the earliest days.

An English bombardelle in the Tower of London, said to be of fourteenth century make, had a box let into the breech. As there was no method of fixing the box, it has been considered a trial pattern. In about 1420 there was a 'holy-water sprinkler', a weapon with four short barrels grouped together but loaded from an opening revealed by a sliding plate at the breech. These were freak ideas but a much more practical firearm is in the Tower of London.

This is a breech-loading harquebus marked 'HR 1537', having a hinged flap which when raised exposes a cavity a few inches long at the rear of the barrel. An inventory taken at the Tower in 1547 when Henry the Eighth died is noteworthy for the number of 'chambered' or breech-loading pieces and also for the fact that many had 'fier lockes'. Several guns mentioned in this list must be those which are still on view in the Tower. In these, the breech had a hinged flap of metal which swung open to permit an iron tube to fit into the barrel. A catch was used to hold the lid down. These inventions were well in advance of their time but they had a drawback. Whereas the modern brass cartridge is soft enough to expand during the explosion to make an even more gas-tight joint, the tapering cone of the ancient iron chamber was no more than a good fit which gradually became more and more loose as the burning gases forced away the metal at the joints. These early gunsmiths were the pioneers, but their names are now lost and only their work remains.

The next attempt at breech-loading was with the wheel-lock weapon, and in about 1600 a type was developed which included a back sight firmly fixed on a circular piece, let into the top of the barrel. When the sight was twisted, the small section unscrewed from the barrel and permitted ammunition to be placed in the cavity. A weapon of this kind is preserved in the United States and the same idea was also applied to flintlock firearms.

An English patent is one issued in 1664 by Abraham Hall. This inventor had his own idea of breech-loading which included 'a hole at the upper end of the breech to receive the charge' and this aperture was closed by a piece of iron 'lying beside the piece', possibly a slide. No further details are available for us to determine exactly how it worked.

Late in the reign of William the Third, a gunsmith called Willmore produced what must be the earliest English breech-loading rifle, with eight grooves making one complete turn in 6 feet. The trigger guard was made as a screw lever which turned round and round before coming off to expose a loading recess. The hindrance of this breech-loader was that it had to be turned up-side-down before it could be loaded. Several gunsmiths produced screw-plugs after Willmore's idea and on the Continent in about 1720 one breech-loader was made with the plug going right through to the top of the barrel—an idea later used by Ferguson.

It is said that the search for a satisfactory breech-loader was not to achieve speed in firing but because a rifled barrel gradually became choked with foul gunpowder and increasingly difficult to load from the muzzle. Thus breech-loading methods were sought and at the same time the old bugbear of escaping gases was slowly overcome by finer precision work and new ideas.

The Tower of London in its vast storehouse of military treasures has examples of rifles from the mid-eighteenth century which are breech-loading. The methods used are various and ingenious but in the main experimental. There is one pattern which has a loose chamber fitting into the barrel, another with the barrel hinged at the breech and released by a second trigger in front of the guard—much in the fashion of modern shotguns. A third type, a seven-grooved rifle, has a lever at the side which when pulled outwards exposes a chamber in the breech-block. No. XXI/257 is marked with the maker's name 'HIRST TOWER HILL', showing that if that gunsmith thought of a valuable improvement he was very close to the place which could take up the idea in a big way.

Marshal Saxe had an *amusette* dated about 1740 which is to be seen in the Paris Musée d'Artillerie. This had a screw-plug and was loaded from below, on the lines of Willmore's patent. These *amusettes* were normally of the wall-piece pattern but some carbines were produced. An Englishman, Warsop, also had a breech-loader which unscrewed from below by means of the guard. This did not go through the top part of the barrel and it had to be completely removed for loading. But none of these methods was put into large scale production. It was not until Ferguson came along and at his own expense and initiative persuaded the British Government to let him equip a body of men armed with his own weapon that a serious advance was made.

Durs Egg, a British gunsmith, made for the Prince Regent a breech-loading rifle on unusual principles. The barrel unscrewed and in going forward on a long screwed plug exposed a hole for the charge. When the barrel was rescrewed the plug gradually closed up the hole. About 1801 a breech-loading flintlock was introduced by Thiess of Nuremberg. This weapon had an iron button below, which raised a block or wedge when struck upwards. This went through the barrel and revealed in it a space to take the charge.

Ten years later an American named Colonel John Hall of Yarmouth, Maine, brought out a patent for a breech-loader which was not only successful but produced in large quantities. Ten thousand of his guns were used against the Red Indians in fighting between 1816 and 1827. In this type the flintlock was placed on top of a block which was pivoted in the breech and could be raised up to be charged from the front end. The flintlock method of firing was used at the Hall Rifle Works at Harper's Ferry until 1832 when it was superseded by the percussion method introduced the previous year.

In 1831 a Frenchman had designed a rampart gun which was a breech-loader and operated by means of a pivoted and slotted chamber held by a movable wedge from behind it. This was a percussion gun, a quick use of the new detonating method. About the same date appeared a Minie Fusil, 'construction David', which opened at the breech by means of a hinged top. This hinged portion included the firing nipple which was worked by a trigger placed well to the rear.

It is interesting to note that even in America muzzle-loading rifles were being produced as late as 1864. Although attempts were made to use the cylinder idea, which had been successfully employed in pistols, it was not successful in a rifled musket. Colt had a muzzle-loading revolving rifle but the gas escape was so great that when one shot was fired all the others were liable to go off in sympathy. Many an American soldier lost his left hand with this weapon. It became customary to load but one shot at a time, and when the American Civil War was over these rifles were offered for sale at 42 cents each.

The decision of the War Office to adopt a breech-loading rifle led to the appointment of a committee. Muzzle-loaders were made avilable for experimental purposes and some fifty ideas were submitted for approval. Most of these used the percussion lock and in the main were cumbersome and tedious to handle. However, Jacob Snider of New York had developed a hinged block and in 1865 this was the pattern officially

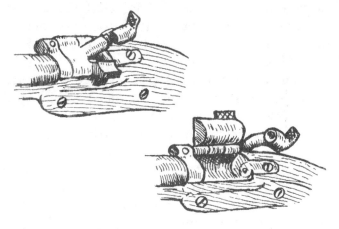

20—Snider action, closed and open.

chosen. It is curious that the idea was very similar to that used on the gun of Henry the Eighth's time already mentioned. Two years later the conversion had begun and the new rifles were being issued to troops. Thus the large supply of obsolete Enfield rifles was put to some use, but the conversion was only meant as a temporary measure. The breech opening was made by means of an oblong section at the end of the barrel. A flanged cover was hinged and opened to the right. The percussion cap holder and ignition hole were part of the cover. This hole was a weakness, improved when a central-fire cartridge was used; but even this, having a brass base and a cartridge paper body, was unsatisfactory and it needed Colonel Boxer of the Royal Laboratory to find the answer with his brass body cartridge. The improved Snider-Enfield had an obliquely placed striker on the breech-block. By now success was permanent and the day of the muzzle-loader was over.

But for all its success the Snider was no more than a compromise. The old percussion rifle converted well but it was necessary to produce a completely new rifle, and in the year that it was taken into use a search began for the perfect weapon. An advertisement from the War Office in October 1866 invited ideas and suggestions. Not only were 120 different fire-arms sent in for consideration but also nearly fifty types of ammunition. Needless to say the ideal weapon was not among them. Inquiries and trials continued over two years and then in February 1869, it was decided to select the best features from several and combine them into the best possible result.

An Austrian, Friedrich von Martini had developed a falling breech and this was accepted. An Edinburgh gunsmith, Alexander Henry had submitted a barrel rifled with seven wide shallow grooves. These ideas were combined and in April 1871 the Martini-Henry rifle was officially adopted.

This was a single-shot rifle and in the trials against fourteen other types achieved fifty-five rounds in three minutes and scored 127 points, leaving the others well down the scale. The new idea of Martini was to have a block operated by a lever below. When this dropped down a channel was available above to permit the entry of the cartridge into the barrel. The return of the lever closed the breech and also left the rifle cocked ready for use. The defect of the Martini was that if the cartridge was not pushed right home, the block would not close; and the method of extracting the cartridge was poor. But here at last was a hammerless gun in regular issue to the British troops.

In 1886 the bore was slightly reduced and the rifling altered at the suggestion of William Ellis Metford. This prolific inventor had worked on the West Country railways before going to India and the East India Railway, just at the time of the Mutiny. He supervised the defences of Calcutta until the Army arrived. When he retired to England he continued his experiment with rifles and hollow based bullets. Ranges up to 1,200 yards were his aim. He comes again into our story when we deal with the magazine rifle. The single-shot rifle had advanced as far as it could and now it was necessary to find a perfect repeating or magazine rifle. It was now the turn of the single-shot rifle to have its days as a military weapon numbered.

4. MULTIPLE FIRE

The idea of multiple fire was an ancient one. The early ribaudequins were of this kind but the aim of some inventors was to combine several barrels in one weapon or stock. The principle of a drum or revolver was tried in the sixteenth century, for the Tower of London has a harquebus with a revolving breech to take four charges. According to Rodolphe Schmidt, author of *Les Armes à Feu Portatives*, a revolving cylinder was used at Berne in 1584 by one Nicholas Zurkinder. The Porte d'Hal Armoury in Brussels had a flintlock musket dated 1632 with six chambers which turned by hand to engage with the single barrel.

Pepys was interested in unusual guns and in July 1662 when he was dining with officers of the Ordnance he observed a gun brought by Sir William Crompton which discharged seven times. The Marquis of Worcester was also a great inventor with many ideas which he does not seem to have carried to a practical stage. In 1663 he noted his discovery of 'ways to discharge a dozen times with no loading, without so much as new priming requisite, or to change it out of one hand to the other'. The Royal Society had presented to it on its meeting in November 1663, 'a very artificial gun' from which its inventor Caspar Calthrop was able to fire seven bullets in succession. At the same period it was noted that Prince Rupert, also a most versatile inventor, had 'contrived a gun exceeding all that hitherto had been invented of that kind, discharging several bullets with ease and without danger. Another inventor, Abraham Hall, took out a patent in 1664 for a gun to repeat seven or eight times. These charges were to be held in the stock of the gun. Unfortunately we know little more about the unusual guns.

Patents were granted in 1681 and 1682 to Charles Cardiffe for 'an expedition with safety to make muskets, carbines, pistols or other small firearms to discharge twice, thrice or more several and distinct shots in a single barrel and lock with once priming and with double lock oftener, reserving one or more shots till occasion offer, which hitherto by none but himself hath been invented or known, the mistery or maine lying in the charge.' Here is another mystery lost forever.

It was not until the nineteenth century that the Americans began the serious work which brought the final result. A repeating arm had been made by C. Jennings who employed a rack with a flintlock. By 1854 Jennings had his extra charges stored in a tube magazine placed below the gun barrel. About the same time Frank Wesson put his Volcanic rifle on the market, and this also had a tube magazine below the barrel. These tubes usually had a strong spring which pressed the rounds of ammunition into place.

The man whose weapon had a wide success about this time was Charles Spencer. Spencer was only 19 when he made the scheme which he successfully applied to both carbine and rifle. His patent was taken out in America in 1860, and when the Civil War began he went to the Government at Washington to sell his invention. After much trouble and persistence he reached the White House and President Lincoln. Lincoln himself tried the weapon, was most favourably impressed and gave orders for its manufacture. Over 94,000 were produced in later months, but numbers up to 103,904 are recorded on existing examples. This weapon had the tube magazine placed in the butt, and the trigger-guard in the form of lever operated a falling block which loaded the cartridge into the breech. Despite its popularity it had a serious defect. The large cartridge of .56 calibre made a strong recoil. The cartridges in the butt magazine had a tendency to strike back on one another and cause an unexpected explosion. This kind of defect was not obviated until the box magazine came into use, with the cartridges placed one above the other.

But before we go on to deal with the magazine rifle we must examine another type of breech-loader, which employed the 'bolt' method of loading.

The defect of the projecting cock or hammer, which caught in clothing or equipment and went off at the wrong moment was obvious to some inventors and attempts were made to get rid of this awkwardly placed piece of mechanism. Weapons without this item were called 'hammerless' and of course had to employ an alternative method of striking or firing. Back in the eighteenth century a hammerless flintlock was produced by Stanislaus Paczelt of Prague, then part of old Bohemia. As early as 1730 this inventor used a piece of metal on the principle of a doorbolt to hold a flint. This was impelled forward by means of a compressed spiral spring. The sparks thus struck entered a central fire touch-hole, another idea born before its time. The whole of the mechanism was enclosed, which in itself was another brilliant thought. It is a pity that the weapon was not produced in great quantities but an example can be seen in the Tower.

It was in about 1814 that Jean Samuel Pauly, a gunsmith of Paris, patented an idea for a central-fire breech-loading gun. This was on the needle-principle, one which was taken up by many nations in later years. The coiled spring, when released, thrust forward a pin or needle of iron. This served to detonate the fulminate now in use. Later the bolt itself was used to push the cartridge into place in the barrel. An English patent on the same principle was taken out in 1831.

Nicholas Dreyse of Sommerda in Germany has been called a pupil of Pauly from whom he may have gained his knowledge and for many years he too had been working on a needle-gun. He had filed a patent as early as 1828 for a method of detonating fulminate by means of a needle, at that time only for use in a muzzle-loaded gun. However, by 1842 the Prussian Army was partly equipped with the needle-gun. As usual there was a defect—they were not gas-tight and soldiers sometimes fired from the hip to protect their eyes. But the Germans knew they had a satisfactory weapon of destruction and it was used until after the Franco-Prussian War. In this campaign the French had their own version of a needle-gun, the Chassepot of 1866 vintage.

Terry and Prince, in 1853 and 1858 respectively, produced their versions of guns on the bolt principle. The Terry rifle only used the bolt to insert the cartridge and it had to be fired by means of a percussion cock, still on the outside. The combination of the two ideas appeared in the needle-gun of 1869 in which the bolt pushed the shot home and being made secure by a quarter turn to the right, was now ready to fire by means of the needle.

The moment was approaching for the British War Office

to adopt the needle and bolt action. James Lee, a Scottish watchmaker who had lived in North America for many years, had designed a bolt-action which was combined with the seven-grooved rifle barrel of Metford—mentioned before. The bore was now fixed at .303 and this combined work came to be known as the Lee-Metford rifle, used for the first time in a standard British weapon the new idea of a magazine. Lee had patented his box-magazine in 1879 and it consisted of an iron case which held five cartridges one above the other. A spring placed below forced the cartridges up towards the breech, and as one was fired and extracted by the bolt the next round rose to the correct place. The bolt pushed the cartridge home and the pin contained in the centre of the bolt detonated the cap. When the bolt was drawn back, the extractors pulled out the used cartridge.

The box-magazine avoided all the accidental explosions that had occurred in the tube or butt magazine where the points pressed on the detonating caps.

It was not until 1883 that a committee was appointed to examine the 'desirability or otherwise of introducing a magazine rifle for naval or military service'. Trials were not made until August 1885 and a decision was held over until February 1887 when the Lee-Burton rifle and the improved Lee rifle came to be tested. This time the latter was accepted and in the late summer of the next year 350 rifles of the new pattern were issued to troops for trial purposes. It was approved, and shown in the *Treatise of Small Arms* published in 1888, but meanwhile other European nations had adopted the box-magazine: Austria in 1886 had one holding five cartridges added to the Mannlicher rifle; Italy in 1887 and Holland in 1888 had converted their single-shot rifles to four-shot magazine types.

The Mark II of the Lee-Metford came out in December 1891 and had a magazine with eight cartridges. In 1895 the rifling was improved by the Royal Small Arms Factory at Enfield and was adopted instead of that of Metford, the new rifle becoming known as the Lee-Enfield. In 1902 a shortened version was produced, known as the Short Lee-Enfield, and this was the weapon in use up to and after the First World War.

Another aid to rapid fire was the clip. It had a much wider use on the Continent than at home. For speed it was found

21—Magazine Lee-Enfield rifle.

convenient to have about five cartridges held in a steel spring clip. These could be arranged over the body in pouches made for the purpose, instead of being loose in a large pouch or mounted single through loops in a bandolier. To load a magazine, a clip was placed over the top opening and the cartridges pressed into place. Ferdinand Ritter van Mannlicher of Steyr in Austria was responsible for this improvement. The Germans introduced this clip to a service rifle in 1888, when it was officially accepted for the Mannlicher gun. The clip was left in the foreign rifles until all shots had been fired and then it dropped out. Larger and more complicated clips were used later, especially on the automatic weapons.

To invent a weapon that discharged all its ammunition automatically was the aim of certain inventors. This meant that instead of the soldier doing most of the work for the firearm, the firearm was to be designed so that once the soldier pressed the trigger, the cartridges would fire themselves until all were expended. There are still debates on the desirability of this type of action, some people holding that it encourages a waste of valuable ammunition without achieving a result. Others hold to the opinion that a single aimed shot has much more value.

The first stage, to being semi-automatic, came fairly easy. This meant extracting the used shot and making the next one ready. The bolt-action had produced this result, but it was manual and not produced by the weapon. It may be that something of this sort had been invented in 1663, according to the description given to us, but it is difficult to say. It was nearly another 200 years later before E. Lindner devised a means by which a piston placed below the gun-barrel was forced by gases to raise a breech-block. There were always more gases created from an explosion than were necessary to drive the bullet forward. The problem was to use them to advantage rather than let them be spent in the recoil which did nothing more than tire or damage the holder. Lindner's method achieved only part of the sought-after result, for the percussion cap had to be fired separately.

Regulus Pilon in 1863 carried the movement a stage farther by using the recoil to cock the hammer. This encouraged many others, but they did not achieve complete success. One who was fascinated by the use of escaping gases was Hiram S. Maxim, who although famous for his machine- or Maxim-guns began his experiments with rifles. The first patent that he took out, in 1883, was to employ the 'blowback' principle to load and a spring action to close the breech, using this method in combination with a revolving magazine. The next year he was working on a rifle with a locking action, but after this he went on to work with machine-guns of which the story can be read in the proper chapter.

Two Englishmen, Paulson and Needham, tried unsuccessfully to convert the Martini-Henry into an automatic rifle. Then both H. A. Schlund and W. Arthur developed a long-recoil breech-type of automatic rifle and took out British patents in 1885. These are many types which cannot be dealt with in this survey, but the semi-automatic principle was well established by the end of the nineteenth century. That is to say, in pulling the trigger a shot was fired and the next one made ready. It needed another pull of the trigger to fire the next shot. Fully-automatic meant that by holding the trigger, shot after shot would fire of its own accord. It is said that the Winchester Arms Company was the first to produce a popular automatic rifle, in 1903. The Winchester repeater was famous from early days, when it was developed on a mechanism designed in 1849 by Messrs. Jennings and Hart, but the new weapon, a .22 rifle, was worked on the blow-back principle. The automatic weapon was unpopular before the 1939-45 war. It was too wasteful according to some, but the Nazis used it extensively and the M.P. (or Machine Pistol) and the Machine Carbine were accepted as successful weapons.

VI

CARBINES

As each type of soldier had a different job to do on the battlefield, so the necessity arose for different weapons. The large gun or harquebus, useful for the infantry-man, was a most difficult weapon to handle on horseback. Its length presented much trouble for the horseman who frequently had the need for two free hands—one for holding the weapon and the other for firing it, to say nothing of the control of the horse.

But efforts were being made to equip the horseman with a satisfactory weapon. Early crude arms included such devices as a rest built on to the pommel of the saddle, or a ring on the breastplate of the rider to hold the tail of the handgun so that it might not escape his grasp. By 1530 a standard weapon had developed—a medium-sized firearm known as a petronel or poitrinal. It was a species of harquebus, somewhat shorter than a musket but of greater calibre. It was carried on a belt over the shoulder so that it could hang freely during a gallop or trot. When halted to fire, the rider brought the petronel around to the front and placed it on his chest or *poitrine*— hence the origin of the name.

According to an ancient French work, the petronels were the inventions of 'the Bandoliers of the Pyrenean mountains' and they were to be made with a 'very strong and quick wheel' —thus showing that the matchlock was deemed too difficult to use on horseback and that the wheel-lock was preferred.

An Order in Council called upon Lancashire in 1586 'to see the said county Furnished with Petronells' because 'Foraine

Forces are made readdie in sundery places, to invade this realme'. The petronel was not considered a British weapon, and an old play refers to it as a 'French petronel' on an occasion when one was mistaken for a dag. The petronels were the ancestors of the carbine and a close connexion for birthplaces might be claimed for both types.

Another horseman's weapon which came into use for a short period was the dragon. This term has been mentioned earlier as a name for the jaws which hold the match, but now it was applied to a particular style of weapon. Markham's *Souldier's Accidence* of 1648 says that 'These dragons are short peeces of sixteen inches the barell and full musquet bore with firelocks or snaphaunces'. The distinction of the dragon at this period was 'an iron work to be carried on a belt of leather, which is buckled over the right shoulder and under the left arm; having a turnell [swivel] of iron with a ring through it which the piece runneth up and downe'. This was the sling which held the firearm and left the mounted infantryman (or dragoon as he was later called—after the weapon) with both hands free.

Among instructions to the troops due to muster in Surrey in James the First's reign is the following information. 'The Armes of a hargobuzier or Dragon which hath succeeded in the place of light horsemen . . . are a good Hargobus or Dragon' —fitted with the ironwork and belt mentioned above.

But dragons soon passed out of use and the carbine became the popular cavalry weapon. Here again is a name for which conflicting origins are suggested. There were Spanish light cavalry men possibly of Moorish origin who were mentioned as 'wild carabineers' and were armed with *carabines* and pistols. These men were later introduced in the French Army as skirmishers and one French authority says that the carbine is a rifled gun derived from the French word *carabiner*, verb to rifle, as of a gun-barrel. But there seems little doubt that the carabineers were named after the firearms and that we must go back farther to the Arabic word *carib* which means a weapon, no doubt from a shorter version of the musket which may have been used by the Moorish horsemen on the Iberian peninsula.

The cost of a carbine in 1631 according to the list of charges to be made by armourers was one pound. The 'carabine' was to have a snaphaunce lock, a belt, swivel and flask complete. No matchlock or wheel-lock carbine is quoted in these lists. The size of a carbine was to be between that of a musket and a pistol.

A later French word of 1678 tells us that there were two types of carbine, 'one ordinary, the other extraordinary'. The first type was described practically as a musket, differing only in the length and the bore of the barrel. But the second was a different affair, with a thicker barrel and 'rayed and channeled from the breech to the muzzle'. The first was fairly common but the rifled carbine was in short supply. In France the wheel-lock was the method chosen for ignition, though England favoured the flintlock. Carbines were in use in Charles the First's reign, but apparently they were of the common variety and Captain Cruso's work on cavalry from about 1630 mentions only that the carbine was the same length as the harquebus, with a different bore taking twenty-four bullets to the pound instead of the seventeen as commonly used.

At the Restoration of King Charles the Second all the troops of Life Guards had carbines. These could hardly have been rifled carbines, as at a slightly later date the Mounted Body Guard of the King of France had but eight rifled carbines in each troop. Regiments of horse raised in England were also given carbines and one such body raised in 1685 were known as the Carabineers, by which title they are still known today although in the Royal Armoured Corps.

A letter written in 1666 by Sir W. Temple noted that the Hungarian mercenaries he saw in Germany had had screwed guns hanging from their backs. These shot a bullet 'the bigness of a large pea' up to the range of 200 yards into a target no wider than a crown piece.

The Duke of Albemarle's *Printed Observations*, published in 1671 after his death, advocated for a horseman 'a carbine, or a musquet barrel of the length of a carbine barrel, well stocked, with a snaphaunce, the which I hold to be much better than a carbine for service'. This preference for a carbine fitted with a flintlock shows that abroad the wheel-lock was normally used with a carbine. A regulation of 1680 ruled that the carbine barrels were to be of the same length as those of a fusil, 3 feet 2 inches. It would appear that the continental carbines were different from the English ones because they were called *à canon brisée* which meant that they were 'broken' or could come into two pieces to go into the holster or even load.

The cost of carbines issued to English Regiments of Horse in 1702 was 26 shillings each, which suggests that they were not of the expensive rifled kind. In a list of the weapons in the Great Store Room of Fort William Henry were '189 firelocks or carbines for Dragoons'; which still seems to indicate that rifled ones were not in store, for such valuable pieces would not have been grouped with the common material.

The cavalry in the British Army seems to have been given almost any weapon that could be passed on without too much protest, including cut-down infantry patterns. In 1772 it was suggested, as new carbines were to be made, that they should be of one pattern as several types had been in use. A further appeal was made, this time for a rifled barrel carbine 'as they apprehend it may be well worth considering if rifled barrels for the Light Dragoons will not be essentially useful for His Majesty's service'. The *Discipline of the Light Horse* published in 1778 mentions that the Light Dragoons carried a carbine 2 feet 5 inches long in the barrel.

In 1786 six different types of carbines were sent to five Light Dragoon Regiments for experimental purposes. There were three lengths of barrels— 2 feet 4 inches; 2 feet 9 inches, and 3 feet 1 inch. Rifled versions were sent as well as smooth-bore ones. After due time, the various commanding officers made their reports which were by no means unanimous. Three preferred the shortest barrel, one the medium size and the last the long barrel. As to rifling, four of them expressed their preference but the other thought that the smooth-bore would be easiest to keep clean. After due deliberation the Board of General Officers published their comments which gave 'a preference to the shortest rifled barrel (viz. of the length of 2 feet 4 inches)' as the best adapted for the service, and in 1788 these were issued to regiments then being converted to Dragoon Guards.

But the pattern of carbines approved in an order of June 1796 appears to have reverted again to the smooth-bore. These were to have a barrel 26 inches long and were issued to both heavy and light cavalry. Until new carbines could be made the old Dragon firelock was to be cut down and used with a 15-inch bayonet.

The carbine in use at the beginning of the nineteenth century had a 21-inch barrel with a curved bar to take a sliding ring by which it was attached to the carbine belt. Early in 1806 the Board of Ordnance found that the pattern in use, the Elliot, was 'deficient' and made no further issue. It appears that its ramrod fell out and so, late in 1806, the Paget carbine was introduced. In the Peninsular War, the Hussars found much need of their carbines. The Paget Light Cavalry carbine

22—Early nineteenth-century carbine.

was most popular. The ramrod difficulty was overcome by a swivel. The Tenth Hussars in 1802 had a carbine with a pistol-grip which they changed in 1806 for a new pattern, possibly the Paget. Despite the popularity rifled carbines were not issued generally to the army. The Eighth Light Dragoons in India in 1821 had only 82 rifles out of 668 carbines, all but the rifles having been issued in 1806 to another regiment: so we see how long the old material was kept in use.

The next pattern issued in the twenties was only 15 inches long in the barrel and, though equipped with a back-sight, it was a weapon of little value. Once again in 1826 a plea went out for swivels to be used on carbines, so it looks as though the old patterns had disappeared. In 1834 there were three sizes of carbines in use in the British Army. The Household Cavalry had theirs with a barrel of 26 inches, heavy cavalry had 28 inches and the Light Cavalry had only 16 inch barrels. It will be seen that inventors and gunsmiths had little opportunity to show their virtues in this particular field, but their moment was coming.

Even the introduction of the percussion lock brought little change, but for the first time the service carbine was given a folding back-sight. The old smooth-bore flintlock carbine was converted to a percussion lock in 1840 and became known as the 'Victoria'. This Victoria carbine was in use as a muzzle-loader for the next seventeen years.

Between 1856 and 1863 several breech-loading carbines were introduced experimentally in the British cavalry. Two of these were English types—the Terry and the Westley-Richards. The Terry rifle operated by means of a lever at the breech end of the barrel and fired by means of an exterior percussion cap. The Westley-Richard had a breech-block hinged to rise vertically by means of a long 'tail', and it fired by means of the percussion lock. When the Snider replaced this weapon in the regular cavalry it was given to yeomanry regiments. Other patterns tried experimentally, including the American Sharp carbine, were taken into the British Army for a short time but all were declared obsolete in 1868.

In December 1861 a muzzle-loading carbine of five grooves was introduced for the East Indian Government, and this was chosen to be converted on the Snider principle in 1867. The barrel was now 2 feet long.

The Martini-Henry was also produced as a seven-grooved carbine and in 1877 replaced the Snider which in its turn was relegated to Volunteers, Yeomanry and the Royal Irish constabulary. The Martini-Metford cavalry carbine which appeared in 1892 was converted from the Martini-Henry. The Magazine Lee-Metford of 1894 had seven grooves and was a .303 bore. The development of this and similar types are given in the chapter on rifles; they varied from their parent in length rather than any radical change of feature.

VII

PISTOLS AND REVOLVERS

~~~~~~

I. SINGLE SHOT

Wᴇ do not know the origin of the pistol. Sir James Turner, writing in his *Pallas Armata* of 1683 says that Camillo Vitelli invented it in Pistoia, when Henry the Eighth reigned in England. Proof of this is not strong although we know the pistol was claimed to be in common use in Germany by 1512.

Napoleon the Third in his monumental work on artillery says the name was derived from the calibre. He quotes a sixteenth-century account which tells of balls as small as a pistole—a small piece of money. It must be pointed out that although the diameter of the coin remained the same, the calibre of the pistol varied. Support for the coin theory can be given by another example. The Germans had a small pocket pistol known as the tercerole, and there was also a small Italian coin known as a terzarolo which had a diameter just under half an inch. The coincidence is interesting. Unfortunately the gold pistole is known to be an inch or more across, rather a large bore for a pistol as a weapon. Francis Grose, the English antiquarian, is frank in his statement. He says of pistols that he knew not the inventor; 'it is the workmen themselves who have improved upon these arms and rendered them more simple'.

Some writers have suggested that the 500 bombards of a palm's length made for Perugio in 1346 were pistols; but it is likely that they were hand cannon attached to long staves. The distinction of a pistol would appear to be that it is a weapon which can be held in one hand for firing.

The first pistols or dags were no more than small harquebusses and fired by the same method—the wheel-lock. Although there is an early exception, it was the invention of the wheellock action which brought about the introduction of the pistol. A long weapon was difficult to fire on horseback, and so also was the match-lock apparatus; thus the invention of a system which could be operated by one hand was the answer to many problems. The German *Reiters* adopted the new weapon with enthusiasm and usually preferred to have two at their saddlebow. These cavalrymen liked their pistols to have a large boss or pommel at the butt, so that when the pistol had fired it could be reversed and used for clubbing the enemy. This brings forward another possible origin of the term. The pistols in early time, and indeed much later as well, were hung on the pommel of the saddle which was also known as a *pistallo*.

The Germans have claimed that they had a flintlock pistol which dates back to 1423, but this seems doubtful because that method of firing was born later. There may be some confusion with the weapons carried at the Siege of Bonifacio in Corsica in 1420. Here the cavalry had a short iron tube ending in a ring of iron. This was said to have been covered with leather and suspended from the saddle. No doubt attempts had been made to find a weapon for horsemen but this does not seem to be very much like a pistol.

Early pistols were not short by modern standards, for one ancient writer, D'Avila, says that they were two palms in length—anything up to eighteen inches. 1544 is stated to be the date of introduction of pistols into England for the cavalry but there is also a statute of Henry the Eighth which said that no firearm should be less than 1 yard in over-all length, butt included. This would appear to eliminate pistols but for the fact that we do know they were in use in Henry's reign—such a progressive monarch was not likely to neglect an opportunity to try anything new. In fact this particular use of pistols was in a novel and cunning way of which there are no examples elsewhere.

1520 is stated to be the date of manufacture and as early as 1542 the Tower of London inventories noted targets of steel

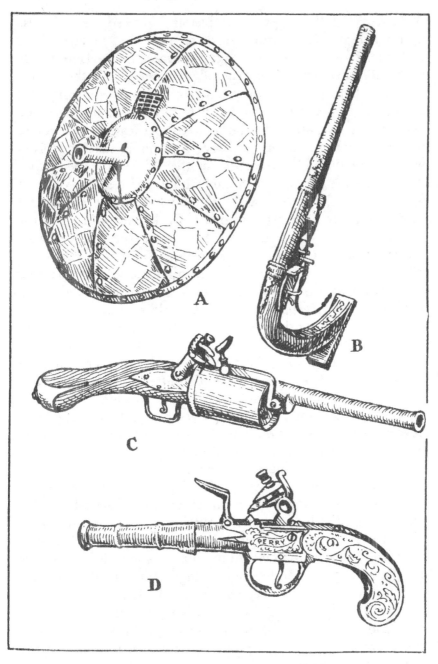

23—A. Pistol shield, Henry the Eighth. B. Elizabethan dag. C. Seventeenth-century revolver. D. Box lock pistol with 'cannon' barrel.

combined with 'little gonnes' or pistols. Up to sixty-six of these unusual items are recorded as being preserved at later dates and one, dated as early as 1520, appeared in a London sale room. As only ten of the originals still remain at the Tower the one offered for sale may have been one of the originals. In any case, it is quite wonderful to have so many preserved and not lost to posterity. The first striking feature that comes to our notice on examining one of them is that the pistol which goes through the centre of the shield is *breech-loading*. A separate metal tube or chamber holds the charge. When it is pushed in the barrel, a 'U'-shaped hinged piece of metal comes down and secures it in place. C. ffoulkes, Master of the Armouries, also claimed that these were the only existing examples of ancient matchlock pistols. The circular wooden shields are about eighteen inches in diameter and are painted red, brown and black or red, black and yellow. There is a small grille in the upper part of the shield so that the firer can observe his target with safety. One of these shields is made with a covering of ten plates of facetted steel. This is possibly the one which was shown to a German visitor in 1606 when he was told that it was 'covered with glittering stones so as to dazzle the enemy with the sun'. These gun-shields were undoubtedly a gallant essay but played no part in the general development of the pistol, which continued to progress rapidly on the Continent at the hands of many gunsmiths, who in fact came to supply England with the new types.

One of these was known as the dag or dagge. The haque or hagbutt had a smaller version known as the demi-hag. One wonders if demi-hag may not have been contracted into dag. This weapon was a wheel-lock firearm which had a butt practically in a half-circle. An account of goods delivered from Flanders in 1559 included 18,000 dags valued at 16s. 8d. each —a vast quantity at a very cheap rate, if they are the normal firearm. Usually the dag was a superior weapon used by noblemen and one of which they were proud, as may be seen from the portraits of Robert Dudley, Earl of Essex and Leicester painted by Zucchero.

A Tower inventory of 1578 noted that 500 pistols were in store, but the Privy Council had to tell the citizens of Norwich six years later to furnish their light horsemen with cases of pistols. These Tower inventories mention unusual variations such as a 'dagge with two peeces in one stocke'. There is also a 'white tacke with fier lock'. The tack was a pistol with a piece of metal on the side to act as a hook to go into a belt. Then there were eleven 'tackes after the fashion of a dagge, with fierlockes and double lockes a pece'. These double locks seem to suggest that the flintlock was being used in conjunction with the pyrites or wheel-lock.

The flintlock was no doubt coming into use in this field for there is an account in 1588 of money paid by the Chamberlain of Norwich to Henry Radoe, a gunsmith, for 'making one of the old pistolls with a snapphaunce and a new stock for it'. The trouble of the wheel-lock's weak spring has been mentioned elsewhere and the advantage of a strong spring and the surety of the flintlock soon led to its adoption in England. It was in the reign of Elizabeth that the second pistol was given to cavalrymen in the place of the estoc or sword.

A breath of things to come appears in a contemporary work of 1594—*The Jewel House* by Sir Hugh Plat, when he tells of a rifled pistol.

The first stage of development after the pyrites lock was the Spanish or Miquelet (Miguelet) lock in which flint was used. The mechanism was conspicuous on the outside of the weapon. A strong mainspring caused a hammer holding the flint to descend on a pivoted pan-cover. The face of the pan-cover was serrated with grooves to make a good sparking surface. The Miquelet took its name from the Spanish or Portuguese marauders who used it.

The lock is sometimes referred to as the demi-battery lock and its invention is credited to Simon Macuart in about 1560. Among the Augsburg gunmakers is the family of Markwordt and two members of this family were invited to Madrid in 1530 by the Emperor Charles the Fifth. The elder was the father Simon. The other, the son, also Simon—el Hijo—who became surnamed Macuarte, is the one who may have produced the new idea. The Miquelet continued in use for many years but had only a local appeal.

The snaphaunce differed by having its mechanism placed inside the woodwork for protection, and is dated back to the same period. The distinction made in modern times between the snaphaunce and the flintlock is that the pan-cover and striking surface were separate in the former but combined in the latter. Actually the term snaphaunce in the seventeenth century was applied indiscriminately to all steel and flint locks.

Pistols achieved a notoriety in the reign of James the First, when the country roads were overrun with robbers and pads who apart from using guns, bows and arrows, usually had pistols. One wonders what kind of pistol might have been so cheap for such a rabble to use; possibly some version of a flintlock.

The list of charges for Armourers which appeared in 1631 has the prices for firelock pistols with a key (which must mean a wheel-lock) as £3 per pair and for horsemen's pistols furnished with snaphaunces, £1 a pair, each with fittings. In 1637 it was stipulated that pistols were not to have barrels under 14 inches in length.

The pistol, although favoured by gentlemen as a personal protection weapon, was also used by ordinary cavalrymen as a shock weapon. In 1632 Captain Cruso published a little work full of illustrations showing how cuirassiers drilled with the pistol. This writer demanded two cases with good firelock pistols hanging at the saddle, and urged that they should have barrels of 18 inches with a bore which would take twenty bullets to the pound. The harquebusier also had a pistol with— as is quaintly recorded—'his purse and his mouth for his bullets'.

The pistol although a common weapon abroad remained a gentleman's weapon in England. During the Civil War noblemen were so proud to possess one that they were painted in their portraits holding a wheel-lock pistol in one hand with the spanner or key for winding in the other. It was Robert Ward, writer of the *Animadversions of Warre* in 1639, directed to officers of the London Trained Bands, who gave the information that the firing of 'our English Pistolls' differed from 'the firelocke Pistoll' in having a back-lock or dog-lock, which was a safety catch to keep the cock back without going off accidentally. But the wheel-lock pistol in England was becoming obsolescent.

Rifling was again considered, and a patent of June 1635 specified rifling, cutting out, and screwing of barrels. A screw-barrelled pistol made by E. Nicholson of London and said to date from about 1650 was made with eight grooves in its foot-long cannon barrel. This would have given a high degree of accuracy for those days. An extra refinement was a swivel attachment by which the barrel when unscrewed was still attached to the butt, an unusual asset for a horseman but very similar to the carbines *à canon brisée* popular in France a little later. There was little need for rifling in a pistol which was mainly used for close fighting. The advantage of a screwed barrel lay in breech-loading.

These pistols with a cannon-shaped barrel were in use in Charles the First's reign. When the barrel was unscrewed, a stout breech-piece was left which could be loaded with powder and shot. To screw the barrel on tightly, slots were placed in it so that a 'key' could be used. One advantage of this system of breech-loading was that the ball could be made slightly larger than the bore, so that when it was fired it made greater compression from the rapidly expanding gases and thus achieved a greater force. The pistol left behind after Naseby by King Charles at Winslow Hall in Leicestershire is of this pattern.

Unfortunately the term 'screwed barrels' has led to confusion as to whether the screwing refers to the place where the barrel joins the breech by means of a screwed thread, or to the rifling made by means of a 'screwing' process. These breech-loading pistols with brass cannon-shaped barrels were popular up to the reign of Queen Anne, and although some had rifling most of them were smooth-bores. There was no necessity for rifled barrels to be used in hand-to-hand fighting and in fact there was little room for such refinements in some pistols of this type which had barrels only a couple of inches long. These little ones were pocket-pistols to be used as personal protection against highwaymen and robbers.

Another kind, called 'waste or Girdle' pistols were of medium length. These had a prong added to the butt which prevented the pistol from falling through the waistbelt. They were made in various styles and were popular with sea-going folk, for pirates as well as peaceful sea-captains. The brass cannon barrel was preferred because it did not rust in the sea air. The blunderbuss or wide mouthed types were also popular at sea because of the weight of shot which could be packed into these weapons. Long range of shot was less important than the greatest effect of spreading shot into a body of men.

The *London Gazette* of 21st/24th January 1677/8 advertised for a lost 'case of screwed barrel pistols' and when Sir George Lockard was murdered in 1689, the murderer was said to have used a 'pocket rifald pistol'. There can be no doubt as to what types are meant in these contemporary notes, and it may be that the confusion arose only in modern writings.

A patent was granted to the Marquis of Worcester in 1661 for 'an invencon to make certayne guns or pistolls which in the tenthe part of one minute may, with a flask contained to that purpose, be recharged—the fourth part of one turn of the barrel which remains fixt, fastening it as forceably and effectually as a dozen threads of a screw.' Further details are not available but it has been suggested that the quarter turn of the barrel exposed a breech opening, into which the powder and ball could be placed. Contemporary weapons that could fit into this category have either a covering sleeve which unscrews or a barrel which rotates. It obviously is not the normal screw-barrel which was well known but maybe a system of broken thread for quick-release.

The length of the barrel in Charles the Second's reign was ordered to be no less than 14 inches and Sir James Turner writing in 1683 says that it may be 2 feet long. A French military work states that the length of military pistol was $2\frac{1}{2}$ feet or thereabouts—very long by modern standards—and for all this length it was expected that the shot 'would carry forty paces more or less', not much of an achievement.

In the early eighteenth century, a new type of lock was introduced and used in conjunction with the screwed cannon barrel. In the past most of the lock was placed on the right-hand side of the pistol and assembled on a single metal plate. The new type was the box-lock, with a plate above as well as on the left side, making a kind of metal box instead of being surrounded partly by wood as in the past. The lock, usually made of brass, now had the cock placed on top with the flash-pan and steel. This too was not a military item, but an overcoat pocket pistol used for personal defence.

Although brass cannon barrels were in use, it was now more

usual to have steel and to remove them, for which short internal grooves were used in conjunction with a fitted key. It is these grooves which are sometimes mistaken for rifling, but as they often only go half an inch deep they would have little practical value. Such English makers as Perry, Archer and Barber made these small box-lock pistols, so popular in Queen Anne's reign.

A variety of all metal pistol was current in Scotland, copied later with advantage by other nations. It had not always been entirely metal and in fact in 1600 had a wood stock. But it was

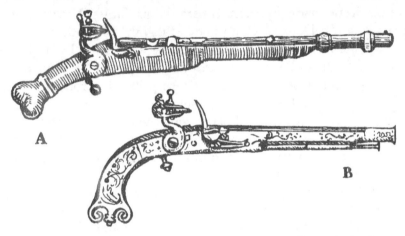

24—A. Scottish pistol, kidney butt. B. Scottish all-metal pistol.

sufficiently a distinctive piece to be sent by James the First as a gift of Scottish workmanship to the Infanta of Spain. The pommel assumed its tulip-shaped appearance by 1620 and then took on the indented kidney silhouette. In 1646 the town of Doune in Stirlingshire was the centre of a flourishing craft where these pistols were made by such well-known gunsmiths as Thomas Cadell and others. By 1650 the wood was encased and at the end of the century the all-metal version with the rams-horn butt was firmly established. At the start of the eighteenth century all-steel flintlocks were part of the dress of any well-dressed Scotsman, and in fact in Europe the all-steel pistol was called *Ecossaise*. Even the well-known but mysterious 'Segallas' make has its place in the Scottish category.

Being a Scottish favourite, it is no wonder that when the

men of the Black Watch were regimented in 1739 they too were issued with the special weapon—made by Bissel, a pistol-maker, said to have flourished in Leith in about 1740–70. They were worn on the front of the body, held in place by means of a long steel tongue running towards the muzzle, a device also used for the pistols of cavalrymen.

The butt of the Highland pistol finished in two curls known as ram's horns, and between them was a knob which when unscrewed revealed a probe for pricking out the touch-hole. Another regulation pattern finishing in a kidney butt was made by John Waters of London. Although normally the all-steel pistols were made by such gunsmiths as James Mickle, John Murdoch of Doune, Campbell MacNab and others, there were some made in brass—for instance, one made by T. Murdoch of Leith to be seen in the Farquharson Collection in the Victoria and Albert Museum. These privately-produced weapons were usually highly ornamented and made without trigger-guards, and the short trigger ended in a large knob. The Scottish pistols were ordered to be laid aside at the beginning of the American Revolution as they were considered unsuitable for bush-fighting.

While the Army strove to produce a standard pistol and bullet, the Navy were content to use almost anything from the most delicate complication purchased privately by an officer down to the most crude affair taken in prize combat. Accuracy of aim was less a necessity than surety of firing and if a large-sized charge could be taken, then so much the better; while brass or gunmetal barrels were sought for their non-ferrous qualities and safety in sea-air. The normal pistol developed slowly. The simple flintlock pistol, like its big sister the 'Brown Bess', remained in general use well into the nineteenth century, despite the attempts at improvements and invention throughout the world. Even the refinement for preventing the loss of the ramrod when loading on horseback was not found until, it is said, Ezekiel Baker produced a swivel which was taken into general use. But attempts had been made at improvement, most important among them being the search for repeating or multi-barrelled weapons.

2. MULTIPLE SHOT

Just as the cannon and musket developed more than one barrel to increase fire power, so at various times the principle was applied to pistols. Double-barrelled pistols were said to have been invented in Munich in 1543, and double *detente* pistols exist having parallel barrels and two sets of locks and triggers. The double-barrelled pistols of the early seventeenth century were made on the same lines as certain larger guns, that is to say, with two barrels each of which had a separate pan, but revolving on a central point, to be fired by a single lock.

One other line of research should first be mentioned—the attempt to put more than one bullet in the same barrel. This may seem a most dangerous practice but it was in popular use at the beginning of the seventeenth century. Two charges and two shots were loaded into the one barrel, and spaced so as to fire by means of two flint or wheel-locks. The foremost lock had to be fired first, and then the second, to complete a somewhat risky business. Apart from man-made error of choosing the wrong trigger first, double-loading involved a risk that burning gases from the first shot might set off the second. For all that, the idea persisted and even percussion pistols on the same plan are known as late as the middle of the nineteenth century, when the Lindsay pistol was made. This had two hammers at the breech-end but a single trigger. The first pull discharged the first shot, and the next pull the second shot.

The earliest multiple single-hand firearm preserved in England is said to be the snaphaunce pistol in the Royal United Services Museum in Whitehall. This contains many features which are part of the revolver as we know it today. It has a brass cylinder with six chambers, each having a separate flash-pan. A brass outer covering protects the cylinder. There is even a device for making the cylinder turn automatically when the cock is pulled back—an idea later rediscovered by Samuel Colt and still used on his Frontier revolver. This weapon weighs over six pounds, is $21\frac{1}{2}$ inches long and has a prong at the side for use as a waist-pistol. Other examples of this pattern are known but the maker can only be guessed, for his work is not signed.

In Charles the Second's reign there were many pistols of the revolver type, and the proceedings of the Royal Society record patterns now lost to us. For example in March 1664 we learn of an invention shown to Prince Rupert. This was 'a pistol shooting as fast as it could be presented and yet to be stopped at pleasure: and wherein the motion of the fire and bullet was made to charge the piece with powder and bullet and to prime it and to bend the cock'. Unfortunately no further details are available and 200 years passed before the idea of using the escaping gases to reload was applied again.

A three-chambered revolver exists marked 'Gorgo, Londini'. It is probable that the piece was made in Italy but marked in London, to avoid trouble with the London gunsmiths. This piece was fitted with a breech-block which had to be rotated by hand. All these early revolvers and repeaters were remarkable for their curiosity rather than for becoming established types. They appear to have been of foreign make and only in fashion a short time, possibly because of the liability of one charge to set off the others.

By the early eighteen-hundreds a more reliable type had been produced. In this the revolving block was brought ready for the next charge by the aid of a lever on the side. In the New York Metropolitan Museum is such a pistol, said to have belonged to Lord Nelson.

A flintlock revolver was designed in about 1809 by an inventor from Boston, Massachusetts. This was Elisha H. Collier, and as he could get no financial support in his own country he came to England where he took out a patent in 1818. In his shop in the Strand he made both revolving pistols and repeating guns. The Collier revolver had five chambers each of which tapered and fitted into shaped barrels. A spring pushed the cylinder home to prevent escape of gases. In some of his examples an automatic primer charged the pan up to ten times.

A Parisian gunsmith, Lenormand, also produced in 1815 a revolving pistol with five barrels, and he made a percussion revolver with a double action hammer. One made later by Devisme of Paris had seven barrels and yet another, the Mariette by means of separate barrels screwed into a multi-nippled breech could fire twenty-four shots.

Muzzle-loading was still the accepted principle in pistols but one sign of a general trend towards the revolver was the wide-spread use of the 'pepper-pot' pistol. In a pepper-pot six barrels would form one solid mass which revolved on a central axis and brought the percussion cap to the striker at the top The pull of the trigger raised the striker, made the barrel move through 60 degrees, and then permitted the striker to fall on the cap. The great weight of the central mass called for a saving of weight somewhere and so the barrels were made short, less than three inches long in many cases. So this muzzle-loading pistol was only of value for shooting at short ranges or wide targets.

At first the nipples and percussion caps radiated from the centre of the block, and as each section presented itself at the top a hammer or striker fixed to the butt above the trigger mechanism rose and fell sharply to detonate the cap. To prevent the caps from falling off, a channel went most of the way round the cylindrical block, close enough to do its work without impeding the movement. Later the nipples or caps were placed horizontally, all pointed towards the firer. This called for the old hammer to be turned into an end-striker, a piece which developed into the hammer so well known on later revolvers. The addition of an extension or lug made it possible for the hammer to be cocked by pressure of the thumb.

There were other attempts to lighten the central block, and one Kuchenreuter of Regensburg in about 1840 produced a pistol with a shortened group of chambers to which he added only one barrel, placed in front of the uppermost chamber. A result was achieved, very similar to the Charles the First gun already mentioned above. The front barrel was connected to the butt by an 'L'-shaped metal piece which went below the revolving section. The cylinder was now made with an axis held at both ends, instead of a single end as previously.

By the middle of the century, Baker had also produced a rifled revolver on similar principles.

The pepper-pots, as they became obsolete, were often converted to the new plan by having their solid blocks cut down and a single barrel added. This makes for confusion in identifying old converted weapons.

But before the revolver system claimed the field, other

inventors were trying out their ideas. There was Sharp's Protector pistol of 1859 which had four barrels, and a single firing pin which moved by ratchet on to the next charge after being fired. There was the Marston pistol which had three barrels one above the other, fired by a pin which moved from top to bottom on the pull of the trigger. Even the early Remington pistols had four or five barrels, some turning on a block. A striking effort was the Jane Harmonica with ten barrels; this pistol brings back thoughts of the medieval orgelgeschütze. These ten barrels were placed side by side and the whole striking mechanism moved along to a fresh barrel after the double action trigger was fired. Lancaster in England produced a pistol with four barrels and in this example the striker moved around.

But to return to the true revolver. It is said that Colt was still in his teens when as early as 1830 he made a pattern for his six-shooter. It was on the ship *Corlo* bound for Calcutta from Boston that he passed his time whittling away in wood a pattern for his ideal pistol. Although the ship's captain laughed at his result, the new pistol was in production six years later at the Patterson, New Jersey, factory of the Patent Firearms Manufacturing Company. Colt's specification of 1835 claimed the ratchet movement as a special feature but Twigg, Hunter and other makers had produced much earlier, flintlock revolvers which turned by hand, on a ratchet.

The revolver pistol was on the right path of development when Samuel Colt took out patents between 1835 and 1847. When he came to Pimlico in 1851 to make revolvers, he progressed little farther than making a few for Indian service. His weapons had been popular in the United States but were not generally adopted in the British Army. His first model had been made for him by a gunsmith of Connecticut, called Anson Chase. But because of the proximity of the firing nipples, when one was fired the others all followed suit. The inventor soon corrected this error and the resulting weapon achieved an appearance very similar to the single-action Army type still made today. Single-action means that when the hammer is pulled back by the thumb, the chamber revolves part of the way and brings the next bullet up to its place in the barrel. The pulling of the trigger was necessary to fire the bullet. In a double action gun, the trigger both fired the shot and set the next charge ready.

Robert Adams, a London gunsmith, was responsible for bringing out in England a series of revolvers. He was associated with the Deane and Adams .436 pistol which was patented in 1851 and shown at the Great Exhibition in Hyde Park. According to the *Text Book of Small Arms* published in 1863 it was called a standard weapon. It had one very good feature— the addition of a strap above the cylinder which did away with the weakness of previous revolvers and produced the first solid-frame revolver. It was a mass-produced weapon, like the Colt, and thus a rivalry sprang up between the two firms. The Small Arms Committee approved the Deane and Adams pistol and it was taken up in this country as well as by the East India Company for their cavalry.

Trials at Woolwich just before the outbreak of the Crimean War encouraged the Government to order up to 40,000 Colt pistols, but the Adams pistol had its adherents who not only used it during the Crimean War but spoke highly in its favour afterwards. In 1855 the Beaumont double-action was added to the Adams pistol and made it much in demand. Then the addition of a hinged hammer gave way to a more powerful one and at last in 1856 the British Government officially adopted the Adams pistol. Recognition of their rival's pistol was too much for the London factory of Messrs. Colt, and they concentrated their efforts afterwards in their American factory, leaving to the English firm a clear field. However, the *Text Book of Small Arms*, 1863, notes that both the .436 Adams Pistol and the .358 Colt pistol were being used in the Army.

All these pistols had been muzzle-loading but the breech-loading revolver was on its way. The American firm of Smith and Wesson did much to bring this about. As early as 1851 they had been making experiments with various types of cartridges including metal ones. One should note that at this period pistols and revolvers began to take their separate paths of development—the cylinder system of the revolver pistol was not satisfactory for a rifle, nor was the bolt action of the rifle applicable to the pistol. Smith and Wesson used an American patent of 1855 by Rollin White to bore the chambers right through the cylinder and make it possible for breech-loading.

A magazine was attached to the butt and the solid frame of 1861 was replaced about three years later by a tip-up system. This meant that by releasing a catch the barrel and cylinder tipped up forwards, away from the butt and trigger. This tip-up method was copied by other United States firms and later in England by Webley. In England the percussion-cap revolver had held the field until 1863 when the firm of Tranter of Birmingham took out a patent for a breech-loader using rim-fire cartridges. Smith and Wesson had at first used rim-fire cartridges but the introduction of central fire cartridges established the breech-loader. Tranter's revolver held six cartridges which after use were ejected by hand by means of a lever along the barrel which pushed a rod into the chambers. Moore's .30 calibre revolver of 1865 also took a cartridge which was inserted from the front but detonated by a projecting tip at the base. Tranter then brought out his version of a breech-loading revolver which was on the lines of his 1863 rim-fire, with the addition of a simple rod-ejector. A central-fire cartridge had been in use with the Snider rifle but was not satisfactory. Thus when Colonel Boxer brought out his cartridge with an all-brass body, the way was open for improvement.

John Adams, the brother of the inventor mentioned above, patented in October 1867 a breech-loading revolver which was adopted officially by the British Government instead of the Beaumont Adams muzzle-loader. The new pattern was a solid frame pistol with six chambers and had a calibre of .450. After the official acceptance of his revolver, Adams left the London Armoury Company and established his own factory, the Adams Patent Small Arms Company, in the Strand. Others produced their version. Webley in 1868 brought out his solid frame .450 Royal Irish Constabulary revolver, which was adopted in many colonies for their police forces.

Having discovered methods of putting cartridges into a revolver and of firing them, the next process to be perfected was how to get them out when fired. Rod ejectors were simple but not quick, even when made with a lever and rod combined. But the break-down or hinged type of revolver gave an opportunity for a separate plate to be added. Galand and Somerville of London and Paris produced one of the first European types with an extractor in 1878. A lever allowed the magazine and barrel to go forward on a rod, leaving the empty cases on a separate plate. Unfortunately the pistol was not of gastight construction. But the same idea of a plate or segment of a plate added to the breakdown revolver worked well. When the fore part of the revolver was tilted forward, the segment with the used shells rose up and could be easily cleared. The process of developing this action took from 1870 till 1890 but once achieved it remained in use.

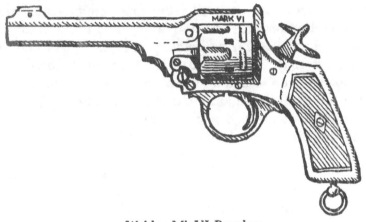

25—Webley Mk.VI Revolver.

The next officially approved revolver for the British Army was the Enfield .455 made at the Small Arms Factory in about 1872 and designed, strangely enough, by an American employee called O. Jones. This was replaced in 1893 by the Webley revolver, which was regarded in England in the same way as the Colt in the United States. The firm originally made muzzle-loading revolvers and produced many useful varieties like the .45 calibre R.I.C. revolver already mentioned, with interesting names such as the British Bull Dog, and the Metropolitan Police, both of 1883, the Army Express and the Chinese Navy revolver. Mark IV which became the standard army revolver in 1893 but the Marks number up to VI. All these revolvers have the cylinder which turns when the trigger is pulled to fire and cock the piece. A variation which appeared in about 1900 was the Webley-Fosbery, a .445 which introduced a new principle of using the recoil to produce almost a fully automatic action.

Lieutent-Colonel G. V. Fosbery V.C. used the Webley as a basis for his idea which involved diagonal grooving on the exterior of the cylinder, which aided the turning. A recoil spring brought the barrel back to its proper place at the same time as the cartridge was extracted. This pattern was the only one on the semi-automatic principle and the later patterns of Webleys returned to normal action.

Although experimental patterns had been made to use the gases or the recoil to perform something more than merely sending forward the projectile, the first commercially sound automatic did not come out until 1893; and this was the Borchardt. It had a magazine holding eight cartridges and used the recoil to push back a bolt which took out the fired round and reloaded. It also had an extra stock which could be added to turn the pistol into a kind of carbine. The Bergman of 1894 and the Mauser of 1898 were German steps along the road, just as the Browning of 1898 for America and the Clair for France showed how the experiments in this field were spreading. Webley-Fosbery, the British pattern, has been mentioned above.

1900 was a turning point in the development of automatic guns, and although the variety of inventions is diverse and mainly foreign, the British put their faith in the revolver. This was the official weapon of the First World War and chosen for the reason that each shot could be controlled to find its target, whereas the automatic could discharge wildly and expend every shot in a few seconds, missing the target and leaving the holder defenceless.

VIII

EXPERIMENTS

~~~~~~

I. WALL PIECES

WALL pieces were a cross between cannon and muskets. They were fired from walls, so the firer did not have to carry his weapon; and they could thus be of unusual length, such as one of 10 feet in the Leichtenstein collection. These wall pieces used in defence of buildings through embrasures or windows sometimes had hooks added to hold the wall and take the recoil. Occasionally, too, they might have the semi-mobile task of defending doorways and passages. We know of *hakenbüchsen* in about 1500 which were used on tripods. These carriages consisted of a wooden trail or plank supported by two front legs. The hook under the firearm which originally took the recoil on the wall performed the same task on the fore-edge of the plank. Phillip the Second of Spain encouraged an increase in size of his troops' muskets, to such an extent that they had to be used on forks or supports and only in sieges.

The cast cannon were now being made so small that it is difficult to say when the falconet ended and the musket began. The tripod stands of these pieces were made more mobile by the addition of two small wheels to the front legs. One serpentine cannon of a mounting of this kind was made in 1614 by Zell Blasi, a Swiss. It was also given a breech-loading apparatus. The leathern cannon of Switzerland too were used with a tripod mounting.

A seventeenth-century falconet exists with its slender barrel perched high on a two-wheeled carriage, like normal cannon but much lighter. More unusual is a flintlock 'wall piece' which has a single large wheel placed in front. The trail consists of two light shafts which could be used for a horse. A *hakenbüchse* of about 1650 by Ditrich Nusbauer in the Vaduz collection has three spidery wooden legs, the front two on small wheels and the hind one supporting an ammunition box.

Marshal Saxe created a light artillery weapon which he called an 'amusette', which was something between a cannon and a blunderbuss. This very long weapon fired a ½-pound lead ball, and was mounted on two wheels but so made that a man could pull it by the shafts. This weapon inspired a piece of artillery which appeared in Dublin in 1761, built on the same lines as the amusette; but it was a breech-loader and, though drawn by one man, could be carried across bogs by two men in the manner of a sedan chair.

2. CURRIERS

Sir John Smith, writing of a Captain Berwick at the siege of Calais in the reign of Queen Mary, stated that 'he doth make no distinction betwixt a currier of warre and a harquebuse'. This currier in the past has puzzled writers but there seems little doubt that it was a weapon for throwing quarreaux or quarrels, those short arrows used at the first invention of firearms. The currier was probably of the same bore as an arquebus but with a longer barrel.

A bill of 1587 quotes 2 shillings for a dozen arrow-heads for muskets. Sir Francis Drake sent a note to the Government on 30th March 1588, asking it to 'forget not the 500 musketts and at least 1,000 arrows'. On 8th April the Privy Council ordered for him 'Muskittes 200, arrowes for the said muskittes with tamkins for each 1,000'. An account by Sir John Hawkins, on his voyage to the South Seas in 1591, mentions the interest that the Spaniards had for the great quantity of short little arrows which were stored on fireships, but that the Spaniards did not know how to use them; 'for that they wanted the tampkings which are first to be driven home before the

26—A. Wallpiece, *circa* 1505. B. Hakenbüchse, *circa* 1650. C. Marshal Saxe's amusette.

arrow be put in'. These musket arrows were only used at sea, sometimes with combustible material in order to set the enemy's rigging on fire.

3. UNUSUAL PISTOLS

There was an unusual kind of pistols known as 'duck's-foot', to be used on mobs and crowds. Officers of law and sea captains apparently found sufficient occasion to need these oddities against mutineers and rioters. Each pistol had four or more barrels placed fanwise and fired by one pull of the trigger. The shot would have spread over a wide area. They were in use in the early nineteenth century with a flintlock action and must have been awkward weapons to stow away.

A seven-barrelled flintlock gun was used in the Navy before Nelson's death, despite other stories. These carbines were designed to fire all barrels at once and to throw a hail of shot in the direction of the upper parts of enemy ships which harboured sharpshooters, to achieve the same kind of effect as case shot or shrapnel.

Pistols of the eighteenth century were sometimes given a small but sharp blade. This was hinged under the fore end of the barrel and folded back below. These sword-pistols were made so that a pull of the trigger released a spring which threw the blade into place. They are sometimes called boarding pistols but seem to have been more employed as shock weapons against highwaymen and foot-pads. A patent was taken out in 1781 by John Waters for a pistol with a bayonet.

A reversal of this idea was also known in the same century and a little later, the pistol-sword. An enemy might be faced by a sword point and take the risk. But a small pistol added to the hand-grip and firing along the side of the blade was a secret and startling weapon. Naval and military swords had these additions, but as a private and not regulation issue.

4. COMBINED WEAPONS

Combination weapons were tried in all ages. One reason seems to have been to keep an old tried favourite in use at the same time as adding a new invention. Another was that when one method was exhausted, a 'second string' might prove effective. The third reason was to possess a shock or secret weapon.

Such a curiosity is the two-handled mace, named in an eighteenth-century survey of the Tower of London as 'King Henry ye 8th Walking Staff'. This cunning weapon has a heavy head with several spikes sticking out at right angles—but also, in the same section, three short guns. This may be the item referred to in the Inventory of 1547 as the 'Great holly water sprincle with three gonnes in the topp'. The term 'holy-water sprinkler' was in use by soldiers from medieval times for other weapons which had spiked heads and an imagined resemblance to the aspergillum of the Roman Catholic Church.

Another version had a solid metal head with four chambers bored out. The loading was made at the lower part of the head, through an aperture revealed by a sliding panel. This example dates from the fifteenth century.

In 1814 Henry Vander Kleft took out a patent for a walking stick which was to contain pistol, powder and ball. In 1828 Isaac Dickson took out a patent for a projectile for a walking stick, and a little later another secret weapon was produced—a cane with a buck-horn handle, which is preserved in America. By unscrewing the brass-covered ferrule the stick is revealed as an octagonal steel barrel. A small hammer concealed in the handle detonated a percussion cap and fired a charge of buckshot.

The 'pole-axe' was an axe of war which seems to have been named either from the long pole on which it was fixed or from the poll or head which it cracked. Examples are known in which the poll-axe has guns let into the butt-end of the shaft which is made with a bell-shaped mouth. The simple touch-hole in the iron barrel suggests an elementary construction which has led the experts to date this weapon from the early sixteenth century. Two halberts in the Doge of Venice's Armoury were made with guns in the staves.

In the seventeenth century each infantry unit had a certain number of musketeers and of pikemen. The pike was the ancient weapon and it would have been ideal to combine it with the firearm. The bayonet was a rudimentary attempt to do this. These short knives could be thrust into the muzzles

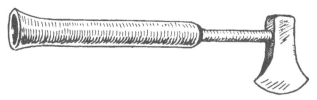

27—Iron hatchet-gun, early fifteenth century.

of the muskets after they had been fired, to make short but cumbersome spears. The presence of the plug bayonet in the muzzle prevented further use of the musket as a firearm and so the socket bayonet had to be introduced, which left the aperture clear. This should have been the ultimate solution but other ideas have been tried. There is in the Royal United Services Museum a flintlock musket with a 30-inch barrel made by Nicholson. By means of a ring let into the fore end of the stock a pike 6 feet 3 inches long could be added. As this removable article lay alongside the barrel it did not interfere with the firing. The head was made in the form of a small spear-head with a cross-bar, and being made detachable could no doubt be worn in a scabbard.

The same museum has another similar weapon, a combined lance and carbine. Once again the carbine is placed on the lower part of the lance butt, and so arranged as to fire freely.

An example right on the fringe of this subject is the Organo del Diavolo. These were little boxes sent by Carrara, the Tyrant of Padua, to the Counts of Breschia. They contained several pistols and were so contrived that when the lids were raised they fired, killing one of the recipients. Pirates chests were also made with the same sort of safeguard to stop prying hands.

5. AIR AND OTHER PROPELLENTS

Although not strictly firearms, airguns are closely allied to the art of gunnery. The replacement of the dangerous explosive by a safer method had for years occupied the mind of inventors. Compressed air seemed to some men to be an answer. The *Windbüchse* invented in 1560 by Guter of Nuremberg opened the way to other continental gunsmiths, mainly Germans. In the Danish Arsenal are air guns and air pistols of 1653 and 1658, in which the Germans placed the pumps in the butts. Although elaborately ornamented the lack of the lock presented a bareness and emptiness on the stock.

Other systems of air guns had the air compressed into copper balls which were put near the place where the bullet was to be discharged. Those in Paris have the air reservoirs placed both below and above the barrel. The latter position was also used for the container of the gun which belonged to that famous huntsman, John Peel. This gun was made by Bates of London in 1778 and could fire more than once without being re-pumped.

A patent was taken out in 1840 for an air gun by John Shaw, and air guns are well known in this country in modern times although forbidden in France. Some regiments in Austria at the end of the eighteenth century were equipped with air guns but the great advances in genuine firearms has left the airgun as little more than a toy.

Air was applied to larger artillery—to a 'Dynamite gun' or, to give it its full title, the 'Zalinski Pneumatic Dynamite Torpedo-Gun'. Lieutenant Zalinski of the 5th United States Artillery actually made the trials and modifications of the original idea produced by an American Engineering firm. The gun tube was 8 inches across and the 145-pound shell was pushed into the tube through a spring controlled gate. The motive power came from two cylinders of compressed air, the upper one connected to the gun by a flexible tube. The second cylinder was the reserve which fed the upper, and was itself kept under compression by means of a steam pump buried in the ground. The dynamite shell was feathered like a dart and had a 50-pound bursting head. The Duke of Cambridge had the Army try one out at Milford Haven but it used up nearly all its ammunition before eventually hitting its mark which was demolished with great effect. But the Zalinski gun and the Craydon gun, also designed to throw dynamite, never came to full fruition.

A steam gun had been thought of earlier in the century. This invention of Jacob Perkins was demonstrated to members of the House of Commons in 1821 and fired 120 bullets a minute. It was described at the time as a frightful means of destruction. It was said that the Perkins steam gun could 'vomit forth as many balls as a battalion'. Perkins had taken out a patent in 1824 for a method of throwing shells and other projectiles by the power of compressed steam. His invention was exhibited at the Adelaide Gallery near St. Martin's in the Fields in 1836. This gallery was devoted to the exhibition of mechanical inventions but was a failure in the same way as the steam gun which failed to make any mark on the progress of war.

Later, when steam as a power was replaced by electricity. an experiment was made with an electric gun. Thomas T. Beningfield, a civil engineer from Jersey, conducted trials of his electric gun at Woolwich in 1845 before high ranking artillery officers. The gun had a barrel which discharged bullets or ball $\frac{5}{8}$ inch across. The machine was on a two-wheeled carriage and could be drawn by a horse at the rate of eight miles an hour. The great asset was that it was said to be able to discharge 1,000 balls per minute, a great speed for those days. Many people were impressed by its performance, including the Duke of Wellington. But the idea was not patented and the inventor would not explain his system. He wanted money immediately, which was not supplied, and the Committee would not submit a report on the gun. Thereafter the whole idea seems to have faded away.

IX

AMMUNITION

~~~~~~

I. GUNPOWDER

ALTHOUGH weapons are the instruments of war, it is actually the ammunition which does damage. The improvement of ammunition has brought about the greatest changes in firearms, and it will be useful to look briefly at this subject.

The idea of 'ammunition' may summon a more exciting meaning than it originally had. The word was French, *l'ammunition* or *la munition* and its Latin root is no more than *munire*—to provide. It referred at first to all supplies, but soon became restricted in its application. The subject divides itself into three main groups: the propellent, the projectile and lastly the igniter.

The invention which set off the great train of discoveries in the field of firearms was gunpowder. Before its discovery all projectiles were thrown by mechanical means such as counterpoise, springs or wound-up cord. But the possibility of chemical propulsion opened up fresh avenues of research. Today gunpowder is merely one means of propulsion through expanding gases. In its day this comparatively simple compound was sufficient for all the immediate needs of firearms. As so often, its inventor is lost in the slow development of an idea and in a mass of conflicting evidence.

For many years the Chinese had been credited with the discovery of gunpowder, mainly from the statements of Jesuit missionaries of the seventeenth and eighteenth centuries. These men had great respect for the antiquity of the Chinese but little real knowledge.

Literal translations of the ancient accounts tell us of man-made thunder and lightning but the use of Greek fire or other wildfire would best meet these exaggerated descriptions. If gunpowder had been known in China in A.D. 85 as stated in Muller's *Treatise of Artillery*, 1780, it is strange that contemporary evidence was not more conclusive. There is one Giovanni de Plan Carpin, an ambassador to the Great Khan in 1246 during the long wars between the Chinese and the Mongols, and although he describes the weapons in detail (he mentions artillery of the ballista and sling type, Greek fire and so forth) he makes no mention of anything resembling gunpowder. Other travellers, such as Marco Polo, also make no mention of it.

The Arabs too, are credited with its use long before the Europeans, but Colonel Hime in *Origins of Artillery* traces this fable back to a Spanish Librarian of the Escurial, Michael Cassil, who in the eighteenth century translated many Eastern manuscripts. An account which is now translated as 'a great machine throwing naphtha balls against a tower' appeared originally as 'a machine which when fire was applied, exploded naphtha and balls against a tower'. The use of cannon is implied in the latter, but only wooden artillery slinging fire-balls is meant in the original.

The three basic ingredients had been known and indeed used in combination, but it was not until the purification of salt-petre that the mixture attained the strength necessary to propel projectiles. It would appear that gunpowder was not a single invention but rather an evolution. The various forms of fire used in warfare were the result of experiments with many ingredients in which charcoal and sulphur were fairly constant. It is strange that no mention of saltpetre is traceable before the thirteenth century. There exist many recipes of Greek and later times but saltpetre is ignored. When it does appear it is in a weak compound and not until it improves in quality does it have any value. However Roger Bacon gave in about the middle of the thirteenth century a method for clarifying saltpetre. It is in his *Epistolae de Secretis Operibus* dedicated to William of Auvergne, Bishop of Paris, that he describes a process of mixing saltpetre and sulphur together with another material—in order that 'tonitruum et corusca-tionem' (thunder and lightning) might be produced when ig-nited. But Bacon felt that all this information was not for the common man and wrote in a fashion not to be understood by the layman. Experts have shown that although the learned monks possessed many secrets, now known and used for the advancement of science, at that early time it was felt best to keep such mighty powers away from the hands of the illiterate or those who might use them unwisely. But even these Latin cryptograms were discovered and the secrets revealed.

Stories that gunpowder had been known in very ancient times to the Chinese, the Greeks, the Arabs or the Hindus can all be discounted by the lack of knowledge of the one important ingredient, saltpetre in its purified form. Various ancient writers compiled lists of recipes for making artificial fire, and it is in such a book that gunpowder was nearly discovered. Marcus Graecus gave some thirty-five recipes in his *Liber Ignium*. This must have been a nom-de-plume, for no true citizen of Greece ever called himself a Greek. Also many editions and additions show that the works extend over a long period of time.

The deductions are that recipes of three different periods were translated from the Arabic by a Spaniard but made with later additions including saltpetre which do not date from before 1225. It is true that some of the recipes go back to the eighth century but only fourteen were suitable for war purposes. Of these nine could be applied to fire, one to fireworks and four to rockets and Roman candles. These last four which call for attention as they all contain the new ingredient saltpetre. Of these, two contain the three ingredients of gunpowder—Salt-petre charcoal and sulphur. The thirty-third recipe is for a flying rocket and the thirteenth makes a kind of fire-cracker. One part of sulphur, two of charcoal and six of saltpetre were to be pounded together on a marble slab. After pulveriz-ing, the compound was to be placed in a *tunica* or sausage-shaped bag. It was to be set off by applying fire to a small hole at one end. If one wished to produce a 'noise' then the *tunica* was to be made short and fat and only partly filled. The case was to be as strong as possible and securely tied at each end with an iron wire. If made long and thin, the result was a rocket.

There was another cleric, Albertus Magnus, a Dominican who became bishop of Ratisbon in 1260 and gave formulae in De Mirabilibus Mundi. His recipe for 'flying fire' is very similar to No. 13 of Marcus Graecus, even to ingredients and the dual use of rocket and cracker. This man died in 1280 long before the alleged invention of Father Schwartz.

Yet another pyrotechnist is Frater Ferrarius or Efferarius of the thirteenth century, who is said to have belonged to one of the northern provinces of Spain. In the Bodleian Library is one of his epistles containing eighty-eight experiments said to have been translated from the Arabic into Latin. It includes a recipe for 'flying fire' made by taking one part of sulphur, two of charcoal of willow or lime-tree, and six of saltpetre to be ground on marble or porphyry. The result could be put in a short and thick case to make thunder or a long and thin one to make a rocket. All these details are very similar to those given by Marcus Graecus and it is suggested that they are by the same person.

A document from the end of Edward the First's reign or just after has a recipe with the proportions of eight parts of salt-petre, two parts of sulphur and one of charcoal, but the interesting point is the description 'de mixtione pulveris as faciendum le Crake'. The crake is obviously a cracker and was used as an instrument of war. With the processed saltpetre, the mixture was now an explosive one, strong enough to propel as well as make a noise. Who made the next vital step—the application as a propellent? The Germans claim Father Schwartz and so his claim must be examined.

For years it has been a popular tale that a German monk, Berthold Schwartz at Mentz in 1320, a chemist, happened to mix some saltpetre with sulphur in a mortar; and that when it was covered with a stone, it accidentally caught fire and blew the stone a considerable distance. But we know that gunpowder was well known in the previous century and one seeks the earliest reference to this monk. His very existence seems to depend on a French document which stated that the King in May 1354 having knowledge of the invention of artillery made in Germany by a monk named Berthold Schwartz, ordered an embargo on the export of copper from France until a decision could be made about French artillery. Sibbald Scott states that this document, from the Bibliothèque Nationale in Paris, bears a date from the seventeenth century. Köhler in his *Kriegswesen* gives a long note on Schwartz and thinks that the alleged contemporary notice is an insertion of the early sixteenth century. Cannon-making seems an unusual trade for a monk, and the fact that copper is to be preserved savours of a later practice rather than an early one when iron was the popular metal.

So it is hard to decide who first made gunpowder, but it was made and put to its deadly use. Then there were attempts to improve its qualities by choosing the best type of ingredients. Saltpetre or nitre is a chemical compound of nitric acid and potash but in ancient times not fully understood. Even as late as 1573 Peter Whitehorne, translating from Machiavelli's writings, says that 'saltpetre is a mixture of many substances, gotten with fire and water of dry and dustie ground, or of the flower that groweth out of new walles in sellars, or of that ground which is found lose within tombes or desolate caves'.

In some parts of the world, India and Spain for example, it is found in its natural state but normally it was cleansed into free potash and nitrate of potash.

Sulphur comes from volcanic countries, chiefly from Sicily. Charcoal was made from light woods such as alder and willow, because they produce a better carbon than the heavy woods.

The ingredients were roughly broken up and mixed together but a thorough grinding in a powdermill was necessary, taking anything from one to six hours work. The resultant powder was very fine in texture, like a flour and usually known as 'serpentine'. This compound worked well enough with a musket or as a primer but not so well in cannon. The finer the powder the quicker it burnt and did not build up the needed rate of expansion. But a way to overcome that problem was found.

A process known as 'corning' was introduced in the fifteenth century and made the finely mealed powder form into larger grains. The larger the bore of the cannon, so much larger were made the grains of powder, and in 1598 some powder was made the size of a pea. This had to be rammed softly so that it was not damaged.

There were strange ideas of adding strength to the powder but modern thought discredits them and believes that the explosive powers were weakened. Some of these practices included adding one ounce of mercury to each pound of brimstone, sprinkling the powder with wine, including sal ammoniac or the addition of peppercorns.

The 'corning' of gunpowder gave some measure of contentment to artillerymen for a period. The next problem was to eliminate the great clouds of smoke which rolled across a battle-field and which on a still day more and more obscured the opponents as time passed by. The French in 1756 brought out a smokeless powder which contained no sulphur but consisted of 80 per cent saltpetre and 20 per cent charcoal. Another powder known as Cartner's had the addition of 3 per cent sulphur, but these were not the final answer. In fact the answer was not found by juggling the proportions of the three time-honoured ingredients.

2. OTHER PROPELLENTS

Inventors thought that they had found the answer in using fulminates. In 1786 Berthollet, the French chemist who produced explosives for Napoleon, made a chlorate explosive by treating silver to make a fulminate. For once an experiment was too successful. The action of the explosion was exceedingly violent. Gun barrels were not strong enough to direct the gases to the muzzle and blew up. Gunpowder liberates the gases slowly; fulminates act practically instantaneously. The violent explosion shattered the metal every time. About 1799 Howard produced a mercury fulminate but this had the same devastating effect. In fact all the early experiments with fulminates produced the same frustrating experience. An amazing expanding force had been found but it could not be tamed. Continual defeat led to despair and abandonment. It needed the vision of Forsyth to conceive its use as a detonator but that is dealt with in its proper place.

A more scientific approach was made to the old ingredients. It was realized that sulphur and charcoal were the combustible parts, while saltpetre supplied the necessary oxygen to make them burn. If one could find a replacement for saltpetre the mixture might burn more rapidly. It will be remembered that the purification of saltpetre brought it to the pitch where it made the necessary strength for an explosive, but that it could be improved no more.

The first steps towards a new explosive were taken in 1845 when Schönbein treated cellulose with nitric acid and produced a substance known as 'gun-cotton'. Sulphuric acid was also used with cellulose. This new field of discovery was a successful one and in 1846 Schönbein demonstrated his invention at Woolwich where it was used as a smokeless propellent for small arms. Its manufacture was begun at Faversham, well known for its powder-mills, but in 1847 a disastrous explosion wrecked the works. France at about the same time witnessed a similar catastrophe and governments became afraid of the new material. In fact it was some sixteen years before confidence was regained, when partial success came to General von Lenk in Austria. He had the compound made up in bobbins of tightly wound guncotton yarn. By this method the threads could not be packed so close as to keep out all the air, and thus the explosive had the habit of burning unevenly. This did not produce the constant expansion needed in accurate gun-firing.

In 1863 at Waltham Abbey, another long established gunpowder factory, Frederick Abel took up the study of guncotton. He developed a safe method by which a pulp could be compressed into blocks. This was an achievement for the manufacture of gun-cotton, carried with it the risk of spontaneous combustion. Although the new process could be safely used in torpedoes and mines, the material was still porous and liable to unsteady burning as before. Abel returns to our story later.

On the Continent in 1865 Schultze produced a powder mixed with gelatine. This last material when combined with gun-cotton and similar compounds produced a mixture in which the pores were much reduced and thus burnt more steadily. The new propellent was applied to small arms but proved too damaging to rifling and was mainly used in shotguns. This also was the defect of the 'E.C. Powder' produced in 1882 by the company of that name.

Final elimination of the 'pores' was achieved when the mixture was completely gelatinized. The explosive was pressed, rolled or made into cords which retained their shape when the solvent had dried out, yet when ignited burnt steadily layer by layer. It was in 1886 that the French chemist Vieille introduced his *Poudre* 'B' which was also made on these lines, and this became the first smokeless powder to be used in the Lebel rifle. Thus the way was clear for similar nitro-cellulose propellents.

Another line of development was opened by the discovery of nitro-glycerine, by Sobrero at Turin in 1846; but this was in its early days used only as a medicine.

Alfred Nobel, a Swedish engineer, found a method of using it as an explosive in 1859. By 1862 he was making it in Sweden for blasting operations. At first the nitro-glycerine was used in its liquid state, but many accidents occurred and this difficulty was only overcome when it was solidified. In 1867 Nobel had discovered this answer by added an infusorial earth known as Kieselguhr, thus making the product so well known as 'dynamite'. Next Nobel had the idea of dissolving 8 per cent nitro-cellulose in nitro-glycerine, to produce a powerful explosive known as 'blasting gelatine'. This was the introduction of the 'double-base' system. Previously a single-base had been thought sufficient. Later Nobel increased the proportions to nearly equal ones and by using camphor to blend the two explosives produced a material capable of being rolled or cut up into any size. This was patented under the name of 'Ballistite'.

Great Britain had not been slow in exploring this new avenue and an Explosives Committee was formed with Frederick Abel, now a baronet, as president. A smokeless propellent which would burn well and give constant results in its ballistics was sought. Many experiments led to the mixture of the two bases mentioned above, gelatinized with acetone. Mineral jelly was also added to assist the processes and prevent the fouling of the barrel but it was also found to give more stable results. The product was hardened off in the shape of a long cord which gave it the name of 'cordite'. There were so many lawsuits at its introduction that it was given the nickname of 'dis-cordite'.

Many modifications of cordite were made but basically the idea remained the same. During the First World War the scarcity of acetone which was used as a gelating solvent led to its replacement by a mixture of ether and alcohol, and the new composition was named 'cordite RDB'. Also, the British factories could not produce enough cordite explosive and the American equivalent had to be used. This was Dupont No. 16 powder, known as NC2 in the British Army, a single base propellent without nitro-glycerine.

3. PROJECTILES

When gunpowder came to be applied to instruments of war there were already in use, for the wooden artillery, projectiles which could be employed with the new science. One machine used the impact of a bent-back plank of wood to send a heavy iron arrow or dart on its way. These darts were frequently made with imitation feathers of brass and despite all inconvenience of shape were made to work in cannon. The lack of closeness of fit was overcome by having the arrow wrapped in a piece of leather possibly moistened, to reduce in some measure the escaping and wasted gases of the explosion. These darts continued to do good work. Froissart records that in 1377 bolts weighing 200 pounds pierced the walls of Château Audrucq near St. Omer. Arrows were still in use in the currier of the Elizabethan period.

But the most successful projectile was the cannonball, and this too had been in use previously, in the slinging types of wooden artillery and cross-bows. Stone shot was used for the former and lead pellets or small balls for the latter. A French document of 1345 mentions lead shot. Robert de Mildenhall, Keeper of Edward the Third's Wardrobe, noted in his accounts that to Calais on 1st and 2nd September 1346 were sent seventy-three large leaden shot, thirty-one small shot and six pieces of lead. We know that at Tournai in 1346 the cannon of Peter of Bruges fired lead shot weighing two pounds. The Black Prince effectively used fire-balls in cannon when in 1356 he took Romorantin in Berry, after setting on fire the roofs and woodwork prior to smoking out the defenders.

The 1373–4 accounts of John de Sleaford, Clerk of the King's Privy Wardrobe, show that workmen were making lead 'pelottes' for guns at the Tower.

An unusual type of shot was designed by a tinman of Bruges. The elders of the town in 1346 ordered an iron cannon with

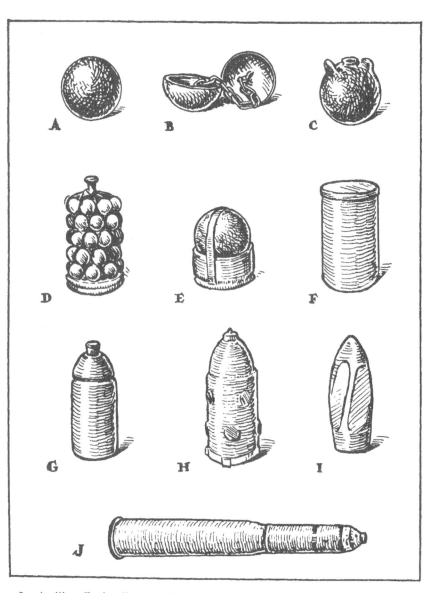

28—Artillery Projectiles—A. Cannon ball. B. Chain shot. C. Shell. D. Grape-shot. E. Shot in wooden shoe. F. Canister shot. G. Armstrong shell. H. Studded shell. I. Whitworth projectile. J. Fixed ammunition.

square bore, which had to have a shot made like a cube weighing 11 pounds. It did its job and was sufficiently effective to pierce the city walls.

Stone cannon balls were also in demand. The Wardrobe accounts of 1382–8 show that Ralph de Halton bought round stones for copper cannon from William Woodward. An artisan employed in this specialized work was paid 6d. a day but, after a decade had passed the wages had risen to 1s. a day.

Stone shot, though they could be produced more readily than metal, tended to break when used against strong walls. By 1350 cast iron shot was also being produced in England, but stone shot remained in use for many more years. Siege artillery did its work well—for instance, at Bamborough in 1464, when the castle defied King Edward; the fortifications were battered to pieces. So demoralizing was the effect of siege artillery that it is recorded of one occasion that the mere arrival of a siege train was sufficient to induce the garrison to surrender.

In 1491 the Venetians at the battle of Taro fired shots of iron, bronze and lead at the French, but by the end of the sixteenth century cast-iron balls were the projectiles in general use. Variations of shot were tried. Stone shot had been covered with lead and the iron shot was made in a variety of shapes. Bar-shot (half balls at either end of an iron bar) and chain shot (iron hemispheres held together by a length of chain) were used against shipping, the idea being to make a wide attack which would bring down rigging and masts.

Spherical shot was in use up to 1875 but experiments had begun with an elongated shape. Once the cylindrical pattern was accepted it was soon found that a pointed nose helped the flight. By the time of the Crimean War, the Armstrong gun was using an elongated shape with the surface covered in lead. This soft covering gripped the grooving of the barrel. The Whitworth gun of the same time had a hexagonal bore and the unusual shape forced on the projectile had planes and twists to conform to that bore.

Rifling was generally applied to cannon and it was decided to reduce the number of grooves to three. To make the shell engage and rotate, studs were placed on the outside. Lead coverings were found liable to strip inside the barrel and foul it after a time. The stud principle worked in some measure but it was found that gases escaped and did not do their full work. A gas check was introduced in 1878. This was in the form of a copper plate attached to the bottom of the shell. The expanding gases made the copper spread and fill the grooves but without the defects of lead. These ideas were later discontinued, for when breech-loading came into use the Vavasseur copper band was applied and became the origin of the driving band as used today.

At about the same period shells were being made of cast steel instead of the cast-iron which had been in use for so long.

The next stage was to make the charge form part of the projectile, in the same way as they had been combined in smallarms. Cordite was the invention, in about 1890, which permitted the quick-firing shell but it was found that fixed charges were not always wanted. So if extra range is needed, additional sections of explosive in silk or other coverings can be added in the breech.

The idea of a single shot from a single gun seemed a waste of effort to some inventors and the alternative of discharging several pellets, small stones, or fragments of metal at one time was tried. Loose shot did not travel very far. When shot was put in a case or canister, it could travel a fair distance before being dispersed. Pebbles or flint were used in a cartridge case on some occasions. In 1410 a gun firing case-shot was noted, as also at the siege of Belgrade in 1439 and of Constantinople in 1453. Canister shot contained many small lead balls in one can but there the projectile might arrive in a complete piece. Grapeshot was designed to overcome this defect. From a disc of wood or metal rose a central stem. Around this were arranged the small iron balls held by cord and an outer cloth cover. The grouping of the small shot gave the name, 'grapeshot'. The exploding gases caused the outer casing to burn away in flight, letting the grape scatter in all directions. A Spanish fortress in 1740 had 2,000 sacks of grape in store. Grape shot was manufactured up to 1868.

The logical advance from canister shot and indiscriminate small shot is to shrapnel and controlled scatter-shot. But before this we must trace the development of incendiary and explosive projectiles.

The idea of a solid shot breaking its way through opposition was a simple one without complications, but other methods than solid weight were not only tried but put into effective use. The idea of heating cannon shot was adopted against shipping and inflammable targets. It was the Ancient Britons who, during Caesar's second invasion in 54 B.C., set the Roman tents on fire by throwing into the camp red-hot balls of clay.

This plan was used again when Stephan Bathory, King of Poland, used heated cannon balls in his siege of Danzig in 1575. The danger of setting off the gunpowder was overcome by using two wads—one dry against the powder, and one wet to stop any burning in the barrel. A thick wad of turf was also a primitive method of insulating the heat from the powder but the charge had to be fired quickly before the heat penetrated. Turf wads were dangerous, as we may see in the Rotunda where a 6-pounder gun is preserved. This was fired in 1783 as the evening gun in St. Lucia in the West Indies, but the damp wad caused it to blow up.

The most successful use of red-shot was by the British artillery besieged in Gibraltar in 1779–83. It was employed so effectively against Spanish ships that a Red-hot Shot medal was issued. On one side of the medal is shown the furnace in which the shot was heated. Two men used a metal carrier to move the shot from furnace to gun. The advantage of red-hot shot was that when it landed on a wooden ship it burnt its way through the decks, with the possibility of setting off a powder magazine or even burning right through the hull. The idea was still in use up to 1870.

It is said that the use of hot shot was superseded in 1850 by a shell invented by a civilian, Martin. This thin-skinned cast iron shell was spherical with an interior lining of loam and shortly before use the shell was filled with molten iron.

Most of these hot-shots became obsolete when naval vessels changed from wooden walls to armour plating. Red-hot shot also had limitations because it cooled so rapidly and was difficult to prepare and handle. Much more effective and sure were the incendiary shells. These containers, originally round, could hold either inflammable or explosive materials and were usually thrown by a mortar. The lineal ancestor is the pot of fire or vase thrown by catapults.

In 1376 the Venetians used these mortar bombs at Jadra,

employing a type which had two hollow hemispheres joined together by a band of iron. Fuzed bombs were also used at the siege of St. Boniface in Corsica in 1421.

In England in 1543 Peter Baude and Collet made mortars which fired cast iron shells which were 'stuffed with fireworks or wildfire'. An iron fuze was screwed into the shell so 'that the firework might be set on fire for to breake in smal pieces, whereof the smallest piece hitting any man would kill or spoile him'. In the famous painting showing the siege of Boulogne in 1544, we see men preparing these bombs.

By 1550 bombs were in common use in mortars. The term 'shell', from the German *Schale*, was coming into popular use and was a closer definition of the actual projectile. The shell assumed more definite features, such as the rings or ears which were used for handling by tongs. The filling neck was now part of the hollow sphere.

At the siege of Gloucester in the Civil War, a Royalist 'grenados' or shell fell in a street near Southgate 'but a woman coming by with a pail of water threw the water thereon and extinguished the phuse thereof so that it brake not'. Cromwell's force attacking Fort Elizabeth in Jersey used 'grenado' shells successfully. A thousand fuzes for shells and 600 hand fuzes were ordered for this occasion. Firemaster Thomas Wright, using a $5\frac{1}{2}$-inch mortar, so well directed the first shot that it hit the Great Tower. By about 1700 these granadoes or shells were being adapted to howitzers as well as mortars.

A type of incendiary shell known as a 'carcasse' had been invented thirty years earlier by a gunner belonging to Christopher van Galen, a Prince Bishop of Munster, famous for his military activities. Carcasses have thick iron shells and are frequently made oblong with several holes to allow the inflammable composition to come out. This mixture consisted of saltpetre, sulphur, rosin, turpentine, sulphide of antimony and tallow. It burnt with extreme violence for from three to twelve minutes, even under water. It was almost impossible to put out and had to be smothered with earth. The defect of the carcase was that when the container was made thin to take the utmost interior filling, the outer walls were made weak with a tendency to blow up in the gun barrel. At the siege of Quebec this defect was overcome by the use of tampions or wads of turf which reduced the shock of the initial explosion. The incendiary bomb with its magnesium filling is the modern counterpart.

Shot had been made to go from gun to ground target to pound, set on fire or damage by explosion. The next stage was to send shot from gun to air and there 'impart directional velocity' to a case of bullets. In 1573 Master Gunner Samuel Zimmerman produced a leaden cylinder with a time fuze in the end, next to the charge in the gun. This fuze ignited when the gun was fired and when the shell was in the air it blew up, spraying out its store of bullets. This was only a passing idea and in fact not practical.

The first successful use of shell fire from guns—before this time shells were projected from mortars or howitzers—was during the siege of Gibraltar in 1779–83. The distance from our batteries to the Spanish lines was up to 2,000 yards and mortar shells could not be made to go so far. It was Captain Mercier of the 39th Regiment of Foot who suggested firing the 5.5-inch shell of the mortar in the 24-pounder gun. To overcome the greater speed in travelling, shorter fuzes were advocated so that the shell would go off at the right time. The idea was tried, and the shells exploded over the head of the enemy working parties. It was a success and although used fully in this campaign was promptly forgotten when it was over.

However the idea was not lost entirely. Henry Shrapnel, an artillery officer, wrote in 1813 that for nearly thirty years he had been conducting experiments which led to his practical use of a gun projectile which he called 'spherical case'. It was in 1792 that the Duke of Richmond had recommended experiments by Lieutenant Shrapnel using 'shot quilted and cased' and shell containing musket balls. The new ammunition was adopted into the service in 1803, and the next year Shrapnel was not only made First Inspector of Artillery but had favourable reports on his new projectiles from Surinam where they were used in an attack. The spherical case filled with bullets and dischargeable in the air was used against the French at the battle of Vimiera in 1808.

The firing charge of Shrapnel's invention was made as large as possible to throw the shell as far as possible. But the walls of the case containing the bullets were made thin, and very little explosive was needed to burst the shell and scatter the contents. Originally known as 'spherical case shot', the name was changed some ten years after the inventor's death to 'Shrapnel'. He received his reward in lifetime and in 1814 was given a pension of £1,200 a year, which he enjoyed until his death in 1842.

The one part which made the shrapnel shell possible was the fuze—and it was also its defect. The evolution of fuzes was just as important as any other part of the art of gunnery. An explosive shell could not be detonated in the same way as its propellent. In early days a piece of slow match was placed in the shell, and it might burn down at the right moment but it could as easily go off too soon or too late. In the early days of fuzes it was sufficient for a fuze to operate when the shell reached its objective. It was thought that a shell which went off in flight was one wasted, but the introduction of shrapnel and case altered that point of view.

Wooden fuzes were in use from the seventeenth century onwards. By 1850 nineteen different time fuzes were in use, of which three were metal. Then Captain Boxer produced his fuze which solved many troubles. This was in the form of a wooden plug containing many small holes. The centre was filled with gun-powder and, when ignited, burnt down to the pre-selected hole and then out into the main explosive. The Boxer fuze remained in use many years and was reliable, but a necessity arose for percussion and concussion fuzes. The first came into action when the projectile hit the ground and the second began working when it received the impact of the exploding propellent. An elementary percussion fuze was the slow match of the spherical bomb, which fell inside when it struck the ground, Surer methods were needed for modern warfare. The first English concussion fuze was invented in 1846 by an Artilleryman, Quartermaster Freeburn, while four years later a percussion fuze was brought out by Commander Moorson.

By the middle of the nineteenth century cannon ammunition was beginning to consolidate all the lines of development into one. The heavy shell was made explosive, to strike its objective with heavy impact, to go off on arrival, to burst in the air or whenever necessary. Refinements were introduced, such as making internal grooves in shells so that they would break up more easily. Lead bullets had a habit of turning into a solid mass when subjected to the heat of the explosion, but hardened lead and coal dust lubrication reduced this difficulty. By 1896 gunpowder was obsolete as a filling for explosive shells. Cordite had been used in 1891 and Lyddite was also adopted. Later such explosives as TNT and Amatol, were used. Complex though the development may have been, it is small compared with recent trends. Projectiles, once thought necessary only for static targets, are designed now to seek out a rapidly moving target and, when close enough, to explode with devastating effect.

4. IGNITERS

One other aspect of the ammunition for cannon must be mentioned—the igniters, the last and essential step for sending the projectile on its way. A piece of metal or wire made red-hot was sufficient in the early days to be plunged in the touch-hole and directly set off the main charge. A small amount of powder on the top of the gun and a flame moved by remote control was the next advance. Then the stick or portfire with its piece of match lent distance and safety to the gunner. The use of a flintlock was not advocated until 1778 when a naval captain, Sir Charles Douglas, had some fitted to the guns on his own ship, the *Duke*, at his own expense and despite the Admiralty. They were a success and officially adopted by the Navy in 1790.

In 1803 Durs Egg, a well-known gunsmith, took out a patent for a type of flintlock pistol to fire a cannon but it was not adopted. The Army kept the portfire, or match on a stick, in use up to 1820. When the fulminates brought the percussion cap to small arms the Navy adopted a percussion tube, but the Army did not follow suit until 1846.

In 1841 a friction tube invented by a Hanoverian officer was tried at Woolwich, but it was rejected. The plan was to have a quill or metal tube containing a small amount of priming powder. This was placed in the priming hole and down into the charge; then by means of a cord or lanyard a piece of material was drawn out rapidly to make a spark and set off the powder. In 1851 Mr. Tozer of the Royal Laboratory produced his version of a friction tube which was officially adopted two years later. When the shell and cartridge were combined the opportunity came for a fulminating detonator to be placed in the base. Ways of detonating by electricity have also been tried but the old method by which a gunner pulls a lanyard can still be seen in modern battles.

5 · SMALL ARMS AMMUNITION

The story of ammunition for small arms follows in some ways the same path as larger artillery, but often we shall find certain processes here long before they became adaptable for cannon.

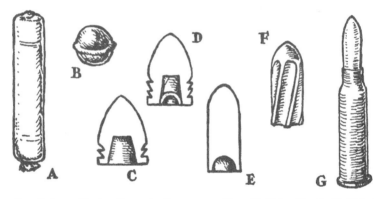

29—Small Arms Projectiles—A. Paper cartridge. B. Belted ball. C. Delvigne bullet. D. Bullet with iron cup. E. Cylindrical bullet. F. Whitworth grooved. G. Cartridge.

It will be remembered that when hand 'gonnes' were first invented they fired lead balls or pellets, and that these remained in use for centuries. Small shot was developed, but used mainly in the hunting field and against robbers and highwaymen. Lead bullets were made in quantities in moulds, but the expert gunman had his own special affair like a pair of pinchers. The bore of guns varied so much that a person who was well away from a gunsmith had to have his own mould. The pincher type of mould had a two-part head which made a cavity for the bullet, and the excess metal from the filling vent was cut off by sharp places on the same mould. Small shot was made by pouring the molten metal through holes in a colander or strainer which was held above a tank of water. The short drop to the water was sufficient to chill the shot. On 10th December 1782 a patent was taken out by William Watts for a method of making 'small shot solid throughout and perfectly globular in form'. The process is said to have arrived in a dream and the method was to drop the molten metal from a great height, which varied according to the size of the shot required. Special towers were needed for this operation and many visitors to London for the 1951 Festival will remember the Shot Tower on the South Bank. This was built in 1826 but its square predecessor was erected in 1789.

In 1743 Benjamin Robbins of the Royal Society advocated an egg-shaped bullet to overcome the defects of the round bullet, but it was not until the nineteenth century that the cylindro-conoidal form of projectile was introduced for the Minie rifle. The twist imparted by rifle grooves made a slight effect on a round bullet to keep it on a steady path but an elongated bullet made a much better flight. Of course a pointed front pierced the air much more readily than a round shape.

Combined with the Minie bullet was an iron cup, to take the impact of the gases, force the soft bullet against the sides of the barrel and make a gas-tight fit.

No matter how far or how strongly a propellent will throw a projectile, it is important that the igniter should act at precisely the right moment. In the middle ages a hot wire was deemed the method to set off gunpowder. Rain, wind and coldness must have made this a risky method. Slow match applied by the hand was a little better. Held in a metal holder or cock as it was in the sixteenth century, there was some certainty that the priming pan would be struck. Pyrites and flint at the end of the century provided a permanent means of preparedness, without relying on weather conditions which could play havoc with burning match. Among the weapons listed in the Gratz arsenal in the late sixteenth century are firearms distinguished as *Radschloss* and *mit Schnapper*. The former seems to indicate the wheel-lock with pyrites, later flint. The revolving wheel produced sparks in the manner of a cigarette-lighter. The idea of getting sparks by means of striking or percussion is said to have been produced in 1596 by Sebastian Hälle with flint and steel. Pyrites was too soft to be struck and so had to give way to flint. Thus pyrites, which Roman soldiers carried on patrol for the purpose of lighting fires, went out of fashion.

Flint remained the standard method of ignition for small arms, until a radical change in the nineteenth century when fulminates were introduced. This had been tried previously as an explosive without success. Pepys as early as 1663 mentions a Dr. Allen he met at a coffee house. This gentleman told him

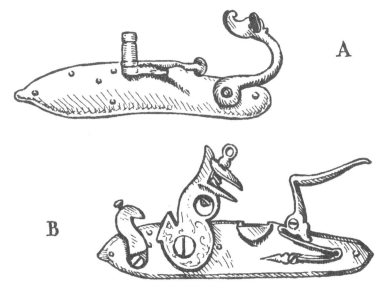

A

B

30—A. Matchlock. B. Flintlock with dog-catch.

of *aurum fulminans*; that if a grain of this substance were put in a silver spoon and then hit, it would blow a hole through the spoon. Members of the Royal Society experimented with the same fulminating salt but little practical application could be made because its action was so violent. Berthollet, a French chemist who woked for Napoleon, tried fulminate of silver but this was of no value either. Howard experimenting at the beginning of the nineteenth century with fulminate of mercury had no success either. Even as a detonator the action was so violent that the explosion blew the gunpowder away without setting it off.

The Rev. J. Alexander Forsyth of Belhelvie, Aberdeenshire, applied himself to its use as a detonator. By 1805 he had built a lock mechanism using mercury fulminate. Two years later he applied for a patent, and although certain people stated that knowledge of this process was previously known, the court of law upheld his application. This was of value to him, for years later he was involved in many lawsuits on this very point. It would appear that this Scottish clergyman applied his powers commercially, for in 1812 Forsyth and Co., Patent Gunmakers, were at 10 Piccadilly, and six years later the address was 8 Leicester Street. The business remained here until 1852 at the least. The system invented by Forsyth was entirely original and used a strong metal flask to feed the detonating powder to the touch-hole. The flask was fixed to the back and when revolved released a small amount of detonator. The great power of the fulminates needed very exact charging apparatus.

Many attempts were made to copy Forsyth's invention, and he had to spend much money suing those who infringed his patent. Joseph Manton, an English gunsmith, brought out an 'original' idea which was little more than a reversal of the clergyman's lock; the fulminate was in the cock and detonated there when it struck the 'anvil'. Manton's first effort was not a success but his second attempt in 1818 was better. He now patented a gun with a copper tube containing the detonating powder. Two years later he improved his idea by placing the tube in the flash hole and hitting it with an axe-shaped hammer. Previously the old hammer head, when it struck, was forced back violently. The narrow axe-edge did not do this, but the tube might flash out to the left or right to the danger of by-standers.

The Forsyth patent was running out and after 1821 many 'inventors' brought out their systems of detonating. One stage of the development had been to place the powder between paper, but the better step was to place the fulminate between thin copper sheets and here a host of claimants made their appeal. Captain Peter Hawker said that he suggested the idea to Joseph Manton the gunsmith about 1818, and this craftsman did make copper caps. Joseph Egg, another famous gunsmith, labelled his products with his own name as the 'Inventor of the Percussion Cap.' The Americans claim that Joshua Shaw of Philadelphia used a steel cap in combination with a fulminate pellet in 1814, but he never patented it, though there is no doubt that two years later he produced an expendible copper cap operated by an external cock.

All these experiments had been conducted with civilian guns and it was not until 1836 that a Woolwich Board approved a percussion gun for the British Army, and took a Brunswick rifle as the first British approved pattern. The touch-hole had been extended to become a stout tube, and the cock altered to a hammer with an overhanging edge to prevent the escape of gases. The fulminating compound was made of three parts of chlorate of potash, two parts of fulminate of mercury and one part of powdered glass.

Meanwhile on the Continent gunsmiths were not content to have the ignition and the projectile in two places. Pauly, a Swiss from Geneva working in Paris in 1806, invented a breechloading musket and then used a paper detonating cap with his cartridge which was fired with a needle. His specification of 1816 said that the plug was so placed as to come between powder and breech to give way to the force of the charge. In 1831 another Paris gunsmith produced a cartridge with a tail containing the detonating powder, which was hit from below by a hammer. In 1847 yet another Parisian patented the pin-fire cartridge which had a metal cap at the base of the cartridge and a wire resting in the cap but sticking out from a hole in the barrel. Guns firing this type of cartridge were shown in the Great Exhibition of 1851 in Hyde Park.

The Needle gun, of which there is an English patent as early as 1831, was a breechloader. The cartridge had a detonator at the base and a needle from the bolt made the necessary impact. Unfortunately the breech was not gas-tight, and the problem was only solved with the invention of the brass cartridge.

An American in the middle of the nineteenth century developed a brass cartridge with a wide rim for extraction, but the vital cap was still outside the gun. In 1852 Charles Lancaster produced a central fire cartridge having the cap in a metal plate. The body of this was still weak but Colonel Boxer of the Royal Laboratory at Woolwich patented a case of thin sheet brass with an iron disk as a base. This new ammunition was used in the Snider rifle. The bottle-necked cartridge came in 1870 from an officer of the American Ordnance Department, and a few years later the drawn brass case was approved by Great Britain.

Such variations of small arms ammunition as incendiary bullets, bullets with explosive heads and similar unpleasant ideas have made little deviation from the main development and need not be described here.

X

GRENADES AND FIRESHIPS

~~~~~~

I. GRENADES

THE grenade as we know it today is very unlike its crude ancestor. In the ninth century, long before gunpowder was invented a kind of grenade was in use. Earthenware vessels were filled with wet quicklime and flung at the enemy. Actual examples of these early earthenware grenades are preserved in Cairo. They were used at Fustat, the ancient capital of Egypt before Cairo was established. It is said that the 'vapour of the quicklime when the pots were broken stifled and choked the enemy and distracted his soldiers'. Various incendiary materials were used in these pots which were thrown by hand. They were not always made of pottery but sometimes of bark, papyrus or glass, the main consideration being that they would break into small pieces and scatter their contents as far as possible. They remained in frequent use up to the end of the thirteenth century.

A work of 1405, Kyeser's *Bellifortus*, shows three pictures of grenades, two of which have spikes like crows' feet. The explosive earthenware grenade was in 1528 used in a battle between the French and the Spanish when an eminent Spaniard called Del Vasto was wounded by a grenade. A few years later we find records that grenades were being made in great quantities at Arles. At the siege of Rouen in 1562 the Comte de Rendan was killed by a grenade. Peter Whitehorne, an English writer of this period, puts on record his knowledge of this weapon. 'Earthen bottles or pottes filled with fire and explosives were used formerly'. He recommended that 'hollow balls of metal as bigge as small boules and a quarter inch thick be cast in moulds, three parts of brass and one part of tin'. The charge was to be three parts of 'serpentine' three parts of fine 'corn powder' and one part of 'rosen'. These ingredients were to be 'quickly thrown' as 'they almost immediately fly into a thousand pieces.'

Meyrick, a Victorian expert, states categorically that grenades were first used in 1594. He may have been quoting Grose, an earlier writer, but it will be seen that they had been in use many years previously. Perhaps the word 'grenade' was coming into use, and again the origin of the word is the subject of argument. Some believe that Grenada was the place of origin, others say the word is derived from pomegranate because of its circular shape. It is interesting to note that Rabelais called these explosive items 'migraines', an abbreviation of *mille graines*, which was a local name for pomegranate as well as being a 'head-ache'.

The grenades of the English Civil War period had the filling hole closed by a wooden plug which had a slot at the side for a piece of slow-fuze. This method of detonating was not a sure one, for it allowed the grenade to go off too early or too late; but this difficulty was overcome by an ingenious 'percussion' igniter, which had a wooden plug with several small holes. A piece of slow-match went through one hole, with a bullet fixed to the end inside the ball. Twigs were put into the other holes, acting as a kind of rudder in the air when the grenade was thrown. The slow match was thus kept to the rear, but when the grenade struck its target or the ground the momentum carried the bullet forward, pulling the end of match from the back into the shell and setting it off. It was recorded that the Roundheads' use of grenadoes at the siege of Colchester much disturbed Lord Lucas's men.

The grenade had been considered a weapon to use on special occasions such as a siege or the storming of trenches or defences. It was a temporary issue but in 1667 the French Army permanently attached four men to each company of infantry to be trained as grenadiers. England and Scotland followed this idea a few years later and even raised troops of horse grenadiers—the Royal Scots Greys owe their distinctive head-dress to this weapon.

In 1678 Evelyn the Diarist visited the army encamped on Hounslow Heath and saw an innovation, 'a new sort of soldiers call'd Granadeers, who were dextrous in flinging hand granados, every one having a pouch full; they had furr'd caps with coped crownes like Janizaries which made them look very fierce and some had long hoods hanging down behind'.

An issue warrant of October 1684 to the Coldstream Guards mentions 106 grenado shells, each having six fuzes. Whether these latter were for practice purposes or because they were often defective in use is not clear. The siege of Athlone in 1691 was notable for the 1,500 grenadiers who forded the Shannon up to their chests in water and yet attacked the town with granadoes, capturing it in one hour afterwards and killing a thousand Irishmen.

A year later a patent was taken out by Philip Dallowe, one of the makers of green glass, for the production of granado shells of glass. Usually in the seventeenth century a grenade was a hollow cast iron sphere with a powder fuze, weighing $2\frac{1}{2}$ pounds. Two from this period preserved in the Tower of London are $2\frac{3}{4}$ inches in diameter.

A military dictionary of 1702 mentions that they were made of pasteboard, wood or tin and lists a new use for them—to make a strong light to reveal the presence of the enemy during night operations.

During the eighteenth century the grenadier still continued in name and was an important part of the infantry organization but the use of the grenade practically died out.

By the Napoleonic times the chief references to grenades are to be found in artillery works. A contemporary painting of 1832 shows a sergeant of the Royal Engineers handling one of these tricky pieces. An artillery handbook of 1839 says that the land service hand grenade weighed 1 pound 13 ounces and could be thrown from 40 to 60 feet.

The Crimean War saw the return of the popularity of the grenade, for this was at times a static war and grenades could be used to dislodge entrenched troops. Both Russians and French at the siege of Sevastopol used grenades. The lack of proper metal shells led the Russians to improvise with glass

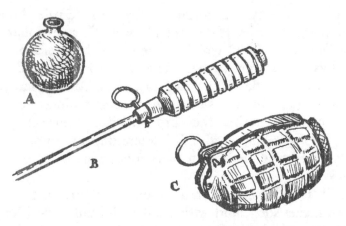

31—A. Eighteenth-century grenade. B. Rifle grenade, First World War. C. Mills hand grenade.

bottles filled with gunpowder and a fuse in the bottle-neck. The modern improvisation of the 'Molotov Cocktail' with the substitution of petrol for powder was a rebirth of the same idea.

The American Civil War provided opportunities for such a weapon to wreak its worst. The British in the Sudan in 1884-5 used cast-iron grenades about the size of tennis balls which operated by the simple means of powder and fuze. The combat which gave the grenade its greatest opportunity to develop was the Russo-Japanese War. The fierce fighting at Port Arthur brought forth improvisations. The Russians used old shell cases by cutting them down to 4 inches and filling them with dynamite or guncotton. The Japanese brought out grenades made from bamboo sticks and even old jam-tins holding up to a pound of gun-cotton. When the fuzes were made too long the opposite side could pick up the grenade and throw it back to the sender. Shortening the fuzes brought quicker ignition but greater danger to the launcher. One answer to this problem was an impact igniter made from a piece of wire and rifle cartridge.

Again it was found necessary to make sure that the grenade travelled in a fixed direction and did not spin around. The Japanese at Mukden used a wooden handle to serve as a guide and they also used a metal cylinder head. A guide tape fluttered behind. The Marten Hale grenade was made on another principle and had an impact mechanism in the base. This

183

could also be mounted on a rod and fired from a rifle. Another feature of the Marten Hale grenade was the steel collar, the twenty-four segments of which broke up at the explosion.

The Aasen was another grenade with a wooden handle with a safety device inside. This was a piece of cord over ten yards long, one end of which was held when the grenade was thrown. At the end of its tether the cord pulled out the safety pin, making the grenade ready for detonating on impact. The Germans used this method in their stick grenades of the First World War.

The British also had stick grenades with throwing handles up to 16 inches long, and with a silk braid tail a yard long to ensure correct flight. The impact detonator was in the form of a sharp point which was jerked into picric acid.

Although the Germans had fixed upon their ideal type of grenade the outbreak of the First World War found the British not so well equipped and some twenty-five patterns were tried. It was found that the long handle had first to be reduced, because it could not be used in narrow trenches. It was cut down to $8\frac{1}{2}$ inches for manual use, but for rifles the Hale Grenades had a rod of 10 inches. This went a distance of 200 yards. The most widely known grenade was the Mills bomb. This oval segmented grenade had no handle but a pin and lever attachment. The removal of the pin did not set the bomb off while the lever was held down, but once the grenade was thrown the lever sprang up and allowed the detonating fuze to work. The explosive was ammonal amatol or alumatol which blew the cast-iron body over a wide area.

Grenades were made for various purposes—one filled with white phosphorus was used to create a dense cloud of white smoke for concealment purposes. Others were used against tanks but more usually grenades have been employed against people.

Apart from manual effort to throw grenades, weapons were invented. One preserved at Goodrich Court had a diameter of 3 inches across the barrel, but the chamber to take the projecting powder was only $1\frac{1}{2}$ inches across. This is often the principle of mortars. The butt showed that it was to be fired from the shoulder and the combination of wheel and match-lock to ignite the charge helps fix the date as Elizabethan.

Another example of grenade discharger is preserved at Woolwich, from a slightly later date. It is of German origin and has a short wide barrel of brass. The diameter is slightly smaller than the previous one and it was fired by means of a wheel-lock. The stock is a long wavy shaft finishing in a T-cross piece to rest on the shoulder or elsewhere. Other examples of these hand-mortars in the Tower of London have flintlocks, so they date from later in the seventeenth century.

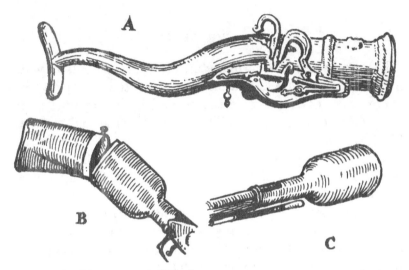

32—Grenade Discharge—A. Hand mortar, seventeenth century. B. Butt-discharger, seventeenth century. C. Muzzle attachment.

By the end of the century the fusil musket was being used to discharge grenades. One method was to use a discharger-cup which fitted on the muzzle by means of a clip or turning device. The other was to use a hollowed space in the butt which was revealed by moving a hinged section. The increased recoil led to the introduction again of a kind of musket-rest. This took the form of a prop hinged just in front of the trigger guard and made so as to fold away under the fusil.

Grenades went out of fashion but the shells thrown by mortars and howitzers were an extension of the grenade method. We do not again hear of grenade throwers until the First World War. It is said that the Germans put into use the cross-bows from the middle ages which they captured in Belgium. In 1915 the French were using improvised catapults to throw their grenades, and later the Germans produced carefully made metal spring catapults. The grenade rifle came back into use, especially on the Western front in the 1917–18 campaign. Spring catapults may have been erratic but at least they possessed the advantage of being silent. With them there was no preliminary explosion to warn the enemy that a grenade was on its way. The trench mortar with its self-propelling shell has taken the place of the grenade thrower.

2. FIRESHIPS

There must have been many unrecorded incidents in which ships were set on fire and launched against the enemy shipping or ports. An early example is recorded by Thucydides at the siege of Syracuse in 413 B.C. The enemy filled an old merchant ship fill of pinewood and faggots. Then they set it on fire and let it drift downwind to the Athenian ships. The Athenians took quick action and not only stopped the fireship but got the fire under control.

Fireships were used in Alexander's siege of Tyre, in Generic's attack on Rome in A.D. 455 and the Crusaders' capture of Constantinople in 1204. But the invention of gunpowder brought into use an extra destroying agent.

An Italian engineer, Frederick Jambolli, made early use of one of these 'infernals' or floating mines at the siege of Antwerp by the Spaniards in 1585. They were exceedingly destructive on this particular occasion and others were encouraged to try them, but without the same success. Nearer home we know of the sterling work that the English fireships did against the Spanish Armada. The British Navy considered the fireship so useful that it was made a permanent part of the fleet. In 1636 each fireship had a master, five petty officers and twenty-five seamen who managed the grappling irons.

The attack on St. Malo on 1st November 1693 was a well-planned expedition led by Commodore Benbow and included four bomb vessels named *Serpent*, *Mortar*, *Firedrake* and *Grenade*. These vessels used mortars to throw bombs, but the greatest damage was achieved by a new galliot of 300 tons named the *Infernal*. This vessel was the idea of a young

Frenchman, Renaud, who some twelve years before had suggested a vessel which might be made as one great bomb. A
vessel 33 feet in length, the floating mine drew 9 feet of water
and was absolutely laden with destructive material. The lowest
part of the ship was ballasted with sand, the lowest deck filled
with 20,000 pounds of gunpowder. The second deck had 600
bombs and carcasses while the third had fifty barrels filled
with all kinds of grenades and fireworks. The upper deck was
covered with old iron cannon and waste metal. A single
engineer carried the vessel under full sail to within pistol shot
of its destination. Despite severe opposition from the shore, he
set fire to his train of powder and left the floating bomb. Its
explosion shook the whole city like an earthquake, uncovered
some 300 houses, threw down the greater part of a wall near
the sea and broke all the glass, china and earthenware for three
leagues about, if one can believe accounts. Strange to say, the
vessel did not completely blow up and it is from the remaining
section that the French were able to give many of these details.

Bomb vessels continued in use throughout the following
century but these were vessels which threw bombs from mortars.
Bomb vessels with such names as *Terror* and *Vesuvius* were
used against the French in 1793 and they also operated in the
Channel, the Mediterranean and even the West Indies.

But fireships were again employed against the French in
1809. In February the French Fleet had anchored in the Basque
Roads. Lord Cochrane successfully sent fireships against their
fleet of eleven and created such panic that all but two ran
aground and out of action.

Fireships were a very expensive luxury and could only be
used on rare occasions. They were superseded when torpedoes
were invented in the late nineteenth century. Driven by electricity
or air, torpedoes are gyroscopically controlled. They have
an explosive head and are still used today. Despite their
expense certain occasions demand some kind of fireship, as at
Zeebrugge. The shore end of the Mole at that seaport had to
be put out of action and two submarines were sent to do it.
C1 and C3 were loaded with several tons of high explosive. In
the action of St. George's Day 1918, C3 was set on its course
by gyro-controlled gear. C1 had broken away from its towing

ship and therefore out of action. The other submarine reached its target and remained an object of derision by the Germans near by until it blew up, blasting away 100 feet of the viaduct and cutting all communications.

A classic example was in 1942 when the destroyer *Campbeltown* was employed to ram the dockgates at St. Nazaire. This ship had five tons of explosives packed into its bows. These were fitted with a delayed action fuze and, of course, the mission was accomplished according to plan.

XI

ROCKETS

~~~~~~

THE modern rocket should be considered less as a fire-arm than a missile, and it is the launcher that takes the place of the firearm, if one accepts the analogy of a bullet and a rifle. However, in its early days the rocket was the complete offensive weapon.

The development of rockets is an interesting trend to follow, for its beginning was even earlier than gunpowder. The method of propulsion is the reverse of firearms. In firearms, the sudden expansion of gases in the confined space of a barrel forces the projectile forwards at a speed which soon decreases to nothing. In rockets, the propellent goes with the missile and the gases discharging backwards do not cause the speed to be reduced but rather to increase.

The application of gunpowder and, later, explosives to the field of artillery has been constant and far-reaching. Rocket propulsion, though desultorily used throughout the centuries, has had to wait until the twentieth century to reach its fullest application. The recent war saw the principle effectively used in bazookas, Z-guns, flying-bombs and jet-aircraft. So important a development which came directly from the use of fire in war cannot be lightly put to one side.

Rockets did not begin as offensive weapons, but rather as toys. The origins go back into the dim pages of the past. It is said that the Roman Emperor Caligula at his notorious feasts and parties had rockets for display.

Throughout the flamboyant writings of the ancient authors

are descriptions of objects which could be taken to represent explosives and rockets. In most cases these turn out to be little more than flying arrows with burning heads. The vital point about rockets is that they propel themselves and are not sent into the air by means of a bow. The Chinese are given credit for inventing them.

There is little doubt that Chinese bowmen frequently used flaming arrows, and various containers were made not only to hold the inflammable mixture but to protect the archer himself. It is said that originally the container on the arrow had the fore-part open to keep the mixture from falling out. But wind resistance and risk of fire-extinction made the designers open the other end instead. A fuze was used to ignite the fire after it left the bow. It is solemnly recorded that at the siege of Pien-King or Kai-Fung-Fu in 1232 the epoch-making event took place. The story is that one archer delayed just a moment too long and the fuze, burning to the mixture, made the arrow take off by itself! Other accounts say that the discovery had been made before and that this siege of 1232 saw the full scale employment of the new shock weapon, the name fe-ee-ho-tsiang meaning arrows of flying fire. The Chinese were fighting against Mongolian or Tartar horsemen and the areas of fire from each arrow is said to have measured ten paces.

The various works on fire-mixtures written in the middle of the thirteenth century give formulas for flying fire which could be placed in a tube. These tubes could be either short and thick for 'thunder-making', or long and thin for a rocket—the *ignis volans*.

A few years later, 1285, an Arab called Hassan Alrammah Nedchureddin in a book on warfare described the rocket, which he called the 'arrow from China'. The fact that he mentioned inclined planes on the ground for launching the missiles shows that he was not thinking of an ordinary arrow. He also describes a large missile to be used on water—his self-moving and burning egg. A pear-shaped body was made with two metal plates. This was filled with naphtha, saltpetre etc. and two poles served as rudders.

An Italian writer, Muratori, tells us that rockets were used at the Battle of Chiozza in 1380. What may well be the first representation of a war rocket by the west, is in the 1405

manuscript of Konrad Kyesar, a German military engineer.
The rocket has a fuze and a launching ramp. The imagination
of European inventors was fired and one, Joanes Fontana, an
Italian, has a drawing of 1520 which shows devices so elaborate
that one wonders whether they may have been only theories.
One long-tailed rocket is made like a bird, the wings of which
were to come into operation once the missile began to fall, thus
carrying it farther on its way. The model of a hare fixed to a
small wheeled platform was also made 'jet-propelled', as were
artificial fish for sea warfare.

Count von Solms in 1547 describes rockets with wings, and
Hanzelet, whose *Traites Militaires* appeared in 1598, describes
and illustrates a military rocket. A crude bundle is lashed to
a stick but the launching apparatus is more elaborate. On a
four-legged stand is a trough grooved for the rocket and capable of being elevated.

Friedrich von Geisslet in Berlin about 1668 projected shells
or bombs into the air by means of 50 and 100-pound rockets.

In 1683 many details were given to the Board of Ordnance
as to the precise duties of the various officers; and the Fire-
Master was to exercise men, paid 2d. a week, then under his
control, to make (among their other work) unfilled paper
rockets. Whether these rockets were to be used in anger is not
clear, for the statement that Sir Martin Beckman was appointed 'comptroller of the Fireworks as well for war as
tryumph', leads one to think that the fireworks may have been
mainly used to celebrate victories, and festive occasions.

There is a bill of 1713 in the Public Records Office which
refers to 'Rocketts' painted red and blue, and also to the twenty-
four rocket chests which were painted in white edged with
black at the cost of 15 shillings each. No doubt the famous
display of Royal Fireworks after a military victory, which
inspired Handel to write his music, contained its share of
military rockets for the Army took an important part in the
celebrations.

In India, the rocket of war had been employed with much
enthusiasm. Hyder Ali of Mysore used hundreds of these fiery
weapons against the British in 1780 at Guntar, where the
Europeans suffered a severe defeat. An Asiatic history of Tippo
Sultan tells us of a mission he sent to the Sultan of Turkey in

1783–4, in which of 'all the presents offered none so much admired as the rockets of which there were none in the country'.

Tippo Sahib, the son of Hyder Ali, knew well the value of these rockets and increased the number of rocket-men from 1,200 to 5,000. These rockets were not made of paper but of iron tubes which weighed from six to twelve pounds. They were guided in flight by bamboo poles 10 feet long and could reach a distance of 'one and a half miles'. For all that they were erratic and only effective on account of their 'salvo' or 'barrage' method of dispatch. Some of these have been preserved at Woolwich. One version says that the iron tubes were 2 feet long and 3 inches in diameter, with a bamboo pole 20 feet long, and that after passing through a man's body they could instantly resume their original force.

As the Mysoreans had been actively aided by many French officers in their wars against the British, it is not surprising that the French probably had some knowledge of rockets. Julien de Belair, a naval officer, after observing their effects returned to France in 1791 and in collaboration with Claude Ruggieri produced a rocket, which in 1798 was used to arm corsairs at Bordeaux.

Shortly after Seringapatam the British authorities felt that there might be something in the idea of rockets and the Ordnance Office applied to the Laboratory at Woolwich Arsenal for people who might be able to make good war rockets. The Laboratory had none and advised the Ordnance Office to apply to the East India Company, as the people 'on the spot' who should know. However, the Company said that they had no one with such knowledge and so the Laboratory had to find the answer from their own staff.

The man who found the solution was William Congreve, who lived from 1772 to 1828. He was the son of Sir William Congreve the first Baronet, Comptroller of the Royal Laboratory at Woolwich. When his father died in 1814 as a Lieutenant-General, he became the second Baronet and also Comptroller. In 1811 he received his first military rank, Lieutenant-Colonel in the Hanoverian Artillery. He published a very full book on his rocket system and tells us he perfected his invention in 1805 when he gave a demonstration before Mr. Pitt and other members of the Government.

Congreve had permission to try out his rockets in action and on 18th November 1805 he went with a small fleet of ten boats which intended to attack Boulogne. Unfortunately a gale arose and disabled five out of the ten boats, and caused the attack to be abandoned. He had been using normal commercial rockets, but finding in 1806 that the paper cases were not suitable, he used sheet-iron and also shortened the sticks to give a better balance. Originally his 6-pound rockets had sticks 7 feet long, and the 12-pound rocket had 9-foot sticks. In the same year he began to make large rockets weighing 32 pounds each, and having a 10-inch head which carried 3,000 yards. He advocated the use of rockets not only for artillery but in all branches of the services.

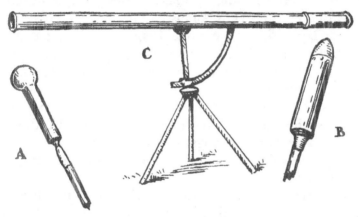

33—A. Congreve rocket. B. Hale's rocket. C. Rocket launcher, late nineteenth century.

The next time Congreve rockets were used on active service they were most successful. In an attack on Boulogne on 8th October 1806, eighteen ships were employed to fire some 200 3-pound rockets; which they achieved in half-an-hour from a distance of 2,300 metres or over 2,400 yards! A contemporary account says 'In about half an hour about 200 rockets were discharged. The dismay and astonishment of the enemy was complete—not a shot was returned—and less than ten minutes after the first discharge the town was discovered to be on fire.' The exact damage done was not recorded, for the French authorities put a strict censorship on the town; and a few days later when Lord Lauderdale and his suite arrived there they were not allowed in the streets but had to travel in closed carriages. No doubt the damage was enough to warrant these strict measures.

In 1807 an attack was made on Copenhagen, when 40,000 rockets and 6,000 bombs created havoc in the city, and led to its surrender after it had been completely destroyed. Rockets were taken to Portugal in 1808 but their performance was erratic, especially when fired from the field carriage. When the Walcheren Expedition sailed to Holland it was intended that rockets should be used to their full scope. But the expedition was a failure despite the rockets which were fired from the five frames of the land batteries under the personal direction of Colonel Congreve, and Flushing was captured after the fighting of 13th–15th August, 1809.

A year later rockets were again employed in the Peninsula, this time against Cadiz and other Spanish towns but their behaviour at Santarem was so unreliable that the Duke of Wellington expressed a preference for the more usual field guns. A staff officer noted in his diary that when rockets were fired to set the French stores alight, 'a high wind brought two of the rockets back amongst the spectators to our no small inconvenience'. Rockets did good service in the crossing of the Adour River in 1813.

It is interesting to note that of all the British forces, the Rocket Brigade alone represented Great Britain at that 'Battle of the Nations' at Leipzig in 1813, where the result was so striking that the remaining artillery officer received the personal thanks of the allied sovereigns and had the Emperor of Russia pin his own Cross of St. Anne on the coat of the artilleryman. Congreve's formidable weapon was said to have paralysed squares of infantry and produced on the enemy an impression of something supernatural, to the extent that a complete French Brigade at Paunsdorf surrendered to the Rocket Brigade. Danzig was also besieged in the same year from the sea, when fire rockets burned the city's supplies and forced its surrender.

Even America saw the rockets in action. When they were employed at Bladensburg, better known as Baltimore, in 1814 at the bombardment of Fort McHenry, the rockets were sufficiently terrifying to inspire a poet. Thus, Francis Scott Key wrote of the 'rocket's red glare' in the American National Anthem. Ladders attached to the ships' masts were the launching ramps, the sails were dampened to prevent them from catching fire and leather was used to protect the unfired rockets.

The Rocket troops came in action again during Napoleon's 'Hundred Days' and although they fired a score of rockets at Quatre Bras and some fifty-eight at Waterloo, they were not entirely successful. The first rocket at Genappes drove the gunners away from a French horse artillery battery but other rockets returned amongst their senders. Those fired on the field of Waterloo had their effect blanketed by the damp grass.

The rocket had now caught the public's imagination and most of the artilleries of Europe imitated the English invention: Russia, Austria, Prussia, Sweden, the Netherlands, Saxony and Sardinia all adopted rockets with secret ingredients. The rocket, having come recently from India to start a fashion, returned now to its own land and both the Bengal and the Madras Horse Artillery adopted Rocket Corps. The Bengal establishment had sixty Europeans mounted on camels, each with eight rockets. Four horse-drawn cars also carried twenty-four rockets each. Although these troops went on expeditions, they were deemed of little use and disbanded in 1821.

Sir William Congreve tells us that he established a factory in 1817 to manufacture rockets which were sent to India for the Rocket troops there. The rocket originally invented by Congreve had a long stick at the side which caused it to take a sideways flight, but in 1819 he improved the design by screwing the stock in the centre. The base of the rocket was given a ring of percolations which allowed the gases to escape.

A useful development of the rocket was its application to life-saving, not only as a distress signal but also as a means of throwing a line to a wrecked vessel. At intervals, rockets were again used for war purposes. In Canada during the 1837 Rebellion, a rocket gave a 'close shave to the Staff Officers'. Some were taken out of store and used at Jellalabad in 1842. In the Crimean War rocket carriages were used at the battle of the Alma.

The Congreve rocket had continued in use for nearly half a century before an inventor produced a challenge. In 1844 William Hale invented a rocket without a stick. He utilized the escape gas as a stabilizer by forcing it to go through a series of holes in the base of the steel cartridge so that it rotated, on the lines of a rifle bullet. These were exhibited at the Paris Exhibition of 1867.

The Naval Brigade used rockets against the Chinese in Canton in 1858 and Rotton's Rocket Brigade was in action there two years later against Sinho, one of the Taku Forts. In the Abyssinian Expedition of 1868 the Naval Rocket Brigade terrified King Theodore with Hale's rockets. In other minor wars and engagements including the Ashanti War, the Zulu War of 1879, Laing's Nek, and the Transvaal War of 1881 both the Navy and Royal Artillery used rockets, the Navy often with 24-pounders from tubes and the Artillery with 9-pounders from troughs.

A rocket battery perished when the Zulu impies overran the British troops at Isandhlwana in 1879. The Navy used rockets in British East Africa in 1895 when the Arabs rebelled against the Sultan of Zanzibar. At Tirah rockets fired against the Afridis were received with contempt and accomplished nothing. Mules were used for these mountain batteries. An encyclopedia of 1906 notes that Hales 9- and 12-pound rockets were still in service but practically obsolete.

The invention of other propellents apart from gunpowder had opened a new field, but pioneers were slow to see it.

When the First World War began, aircraft became offensive weapons, although armed in the earlier stages with nothing more deadly than a revolver. The possibilities of rockets were noted and British, French and Russian airmen used these light fireworks against captive balloons. A French naval officer, Le Prieur, saw the possibilities of the rocket and used four on each side of a biplane. The appearance and principle of propulsion was no more than that of a Congreve rocket. These rockets were ignited electrically from the cockpit. The Germans also used rockets in their static trench warfare. These carried a small anchor on a line and were intended to tear up barbed wire entanglements.

The vast field of rocket propulsion has now expanded into a

major invention covering such a variety of applications as the Bazooka of the Americans, the Z-gun of the British, the Nebelwerfer and flying-bombs of the Germans, the Katouchka of the Russians and the whole range of half-projectiles and half-aircraft still on the secret list. The humble toy of amusement has developed into the means of a way to the stars.

Bibliography

Armouries of the Tower of London, The, C. J. ffoulkes, 1915.
Armoury Hall, The, Royal Danish Arsenal Museum, 1953.
Arms and Armament, C. J. ffoulkes, 1945.
Arms and Armour, A. Demmin, 1911.
Arte Fabrile, A. Petri, 1642.
Artillerist's Manual. F. A. Griffiths, 1839.
Beschreabuq, J. Furttenbech, 1627.
British Army, The, Sir S. D. Scott, 1868.
Catalogue des Armes et Armures, Porte de Hal, 1902.
Cromwell's Army, C. H. Firth, 1921.
De l'Art Militari, F. Vegece, 1536.
De re Militari, R. Valternius, 1534.
Defensive Armour, The, R. C. Clephan, 1900.
Dictionary of Dates, Haydn.
Encyclopaedia Britannica, Ninth edition, (Article).
English Guns and Rifles, J. N. George, 1947.
Etudes sur le Passe et l'Avenir de l'Artillerie, Fave and Napoleon III, 1862, (Article).
Firearms in England in the 14th Century, Prof. T. F. Tout, 1911.
Gun and its Development, The, W. W. Greener, 1910.
Gunfounders of England, The, C. J. ffoulkes, 1937.
Gunpowder and Ammunition, H. W. L. Hime, 1904.
History of Firearms, A, H. B. C. Pollard, 1926.
History of the Art of War in the Middle Ages, Sir C. Oman, 1924.
History of the Royal Regiment of Artillery, 1815–53, H. W. L. Hime, 1908.
Illustre de re Militari, F. Vegetius, 1532.
Les Armes à Feu Portatives, R. Schmidt, 1877.
Machine Gun, The, G. M. Chinn, 1951.
Military Antiquities, F. Grose, 1800.
Official Catalogue of Museum of Artillery, Woolwich, 1906.
Origin of Artillery, The, H. W. L. Hime, 1915.

BIBLIOGRAPHY

Pistols and Revolvers, W. H. B. Smith, 1946.
Projectile Weapons of War etc., J. Scoffern, 1852.
Quellen zur Geschichte des Feuerwaffen, V. G. Essenwein, 1872.
Rifles, W. H. B. Smith, 1948.
Some Historical Uses of Fire as a Weapon of War, 1943.
Textbook of Small Arms 1909, 1929.
Treatise on Military Small Arms, H. Bond, 1884.
Vraye Instruction de l'Artillerie, de Bry, 1614.

The above are a few of the works consulted and they are suggested as further sources for those who wish to study this subject more deeply.

Index